# A MIRACULOUS DRAUGHT OF FISHES

'Simon Peter went up, and drew the net to land
full of great fishes, an hundred and fifty and
three.'
(St John xxi 11)


'There shall be taught in the scole children of
all nacions and countres indifferently to the
Noumber of a cliii according to the noumber
of the setys in the scole.'
(John Colet: *Statuta Paulinae Scholae*)

# A MIRACULOUS
# DRAUGHT OF FISHES

## A History of St Paul's School

A. H. MEAD

To St Paul's School
Common Room,
a society of which
the author is proud to be
a member

Published by James & James
the registered imprint of Landscape Books Ltd
75 Carleton Road, London N7 0ET

First published 1990

**British Library Cataloguing in Publication Data**
Mead, A. H.
A miraculous draught of fishes : a history of St. Paul's School.
1. Great Britain. Schools
I. Title
371.00941

ISBN 0-907383-05-X

Designed by Christine Wood

Originated and printed in Great Britain by
BAS Printers Limited, Over Wallop, Hampshire

Bound in Great Britain by
Hunter & Foulis Ltd, Edinburgh

*Half-title page:* Simon Peter catching the
miraculous draught of fishes: engraving from
*Lays of the Seven Half-Centuries* (1859) by High
Master Kynaston.

*Title page:* Drawing of the fourth school building
at Hammersmith

# CONTENTS

# ACKNOWLEDGEMENTS

My debts of gratitude begin with the Governors and High Master of St Paul's School, who were rash enough to invite me to write this book, and kind enough to give me two terms' leave in which to do it. I thank also the Worshipful Company of Mercers for giving me access to their archives, and their Archivist, Anne Sutton, and Assistant Archivist, Ann Wingfield, for making it easy and pleasant to work there. The Archivist of St Paul's School, Mr Christopher Dean, was equally helpful; he also read the whole text and made many valuable suggestions. The Reverend Stephen Young cheerfully and efficiently shouldered much extra work and responsibility while I was away.

Dr M. K. Lawson, the School Librarian, photographed archival material in the School's collection especially for this book. The scholar's fish beginning each chapter was drawn by Mrs Penny Holmes.

Three scholars kindly allowed me to read in typescript their as yet unpublished work; I am grateful to Dr Susan Brigden (*London and the Reformation*), Dr K. L. Demolin (*Richard Mulcaster and Educational Reform in the Renaissance*) and Dr I. G. Doolittle (*A History of the Mercers' Company 1579–1959*).

I should also like to thank Mr J. A. Allport, the Rt Hon Kenneth Baker MP, Mr R. S. Baldock (Surmaster), Mr Michael Berlin, Mr A. B. Cook (formerly Surmaster), Mr Henry Fearon, Mr J. W. Hele CBE (formerly High Master), Mr R. Davenport Hines, Air Commodore K. Hitchcock CBE, Hamish MacGibbon and Sydney Francis at James & James, Mr Philip McGuinness, Mrs Alix MacKechnie, Mr Michael Prendergast, Mr Robert Silver, Mr P. F. Thomson (formerly Surmaster), Professor J. B. Trapp, Mr J. P. Varcoe, Dr Henry Woudhuysen, and finally and especially my wife Judith, who turned my foul manuscript into a fair typescript with skill, patience and good humour.

# FOREWORD

## *by The Reverend Canon Peter Pilkington*

Hugh Mead was appointed to teach History at St Paul's in 1966 and, having been both archivist and librarian, is uniquely qualified to write about the long history of the school. In the past, some school histories have been antiquarian studies, or pious and narrow surveys of achievement. Hugh Mead has set out to place his book within the wider framework of English history and educational change.

Ideas rather than buildings have always governed the development of St Paul's. There were three schools on its first site in the City, in 1884 came the move to Hammersmith, and finally, in 1968, to Barnes. John Colet's school was a product of the Renaissance, endowed to train able pupils in faith and letters. He set up his school in the City, making a City company the trustees of his foundation, and for four centuries the school existed side by side with the busy commercial and political life of the City of London. John Milton, an Old Pauline, reflected this interplay of idealism and practicality when he wrote 'the end of learning is to repair the ruins of our first parents by regaining to know God aright', but also added: 'I call therefore a complete and generous education that which fits a man to perform justly, skilfully and magnanimously all the offices both private and public of peace and war.'

Colet's foundation has always tried to bridge the gap between religious ideals and secular society. His principle to admit pupils of 'all nacions and countres indifferently' has meant that over the last century the school has not allowed its entry to be governed by confessional restrictions. Hugh Mead shows how the school has attempted to fulfil Colet's ideals through five centuries of change. The book is also a study of people and a community in adversity and triumph, and it captures the individualism and diversity which have always characterized St Paul's.

MARCH 1990

# I

## 'OBVIOUSLY A SCHOOL OF NO IMPORTANCE'

*John Colet*

## BEFORE 1509

*Roger Gale, himself the son of a High Master, presented this illustration to Knight's* Life of Colet. *It shows the bust of the Founder which stood over the High Master's chair, and was found after the Great Fire 'in the Rubbish . . . by a curious Man in the City Antiquities'.*

Although you cannot serve God and Mammon, great cities have never lacked temples to both. In the heart of the City of London stands the Royal Exchange, originally built (in 1566) as a commercial centre for the City by the Old Pauline and Mercer, Sir Thomas Gresham. Gresham was a successful and very hard-headed businessman, a benefactor both of the City and of his livery company, and also of education, science and religion. His benefactions, however, often had awkward strings attached.

Walking west from the Royal Exchange along Poultry and Cheapside, one would have passed, in Gresham's day, the Hall of his company, the Mercers, now set back in Ironmonger Lane, but then with a spacious frontage along Cheapside itself. Merchants and City politicians, the Mercers were already also prominent as managers of educational and religious trusts, the greatest of which forms the subject of this book. From Mercers' Hall, the old cathedral church of St Paul dominated the western roofscape, and was already in practice dedicated not only to the worship of God but also to the use of citizens who found its vast sheltered spaces convenient for pleasure and business. In the shadow of its eastern walls, far too small for its features to stand out with any individuality in Elizabethan street plans, nestled St Paul's School.

About four hundred years after Gresham's death, another Old Pauline, Kenneth Baker, became Secretary of State for Education and Science. He was a reformer, but a reformer faced with conflicting signposts. What are schools for? They are, for pragmatists, to train people who can earn their living with profit to themselves and their country. They are, to idealists, for opening eyes to the world, and the stars, and to what is beyond the stars. In the little world of school the same muddled cult of God and Mammon has gone on as in the great city around it.

Schoolmasters, outside their own little kingdoms, have seldom cut much of a figure. In 1511, Erasmus in Cambridge was trying to recruit staff for St Paul's School, but nobody, he was firmly told, who could earn his living in any other way, would teach boys. Inside the schoolroom it was quite another matter. There the master, enthroned on his chair, became the immedite embodiment of that paternal authority which, already familiar to his pupils in their father at home, reflected the authority of higher beings.

At the upper end of St Paul's School, wrote John Strype, who had been a boy there from 1657 to 1661, 'facing the Door, was a decent *Cathedra*, or Chair placed, somewhat advanced, for the high Master to sit in, when he pleased, and to teach and dictate there'. Over the High Master's chair in Strype's day was 'a lively *Effigies*: (and of exquisite Art) of the head of Dr Colet, cut (as it seemed) either in Stone or Wood'. But John Colet himself had set in that place 'a picture of the boy Jesus, seated, in the attitude of one teaching, and over it an image of God the Father saying "Hear Ye Him". These words', wrote Erasmus, 'were added at my suggestion.' The words come from St Matthew: Jesus, on the high mountain, is revealed for what he is; his garments shine like light; he converses with Moses and Elijah, with the law and the prophets. The law, wrote St Paul in his letter to the Galatians, was our schoolmaster, to bring us unto Christ. The Pauline, Colet prayed in his *Little Prayer to the Boy Jesus*, will learn at school, so to walk in Christ's footsteps in this brief life, that he may be able, by grace, to receive some share in Christ's glory.

A. F. Leach, the great Edwardian pundit of public school history, thought that St Paul's could claim to be founded in 886. If he was right, it is probably older than any other surviving English school, except those attached to the cathedrals of Canterbury and York. But he was not right, as was pointed out with some acerbity and pleasure by Colet's biographer and editor J. H. Lupton (d. 1905) and the School's greatest historian, Sir Michael McDonnell (d. 1956). Leach's date is that of the conquest of London by King Alfred when, Leach assumes, the already ancient obligation of a bishop to maintain a school at his cathedral would have been revived: but it is not certain either that Alfred did conquer London in that year, or that Christianity and the bishopric had previously been extinguished, or that there was any cathedral school at St Paul's at the time. There may have been one much earlier: there was a bishop of London in the fourth century. There may not have been one until much later: the first schoolmaster whose name is known – Leach calls him the first High Master – was Durandus, a prebendary of St Paul's in 1103. Even he is doubted by McDonnell, but Magister Durandus de Anglia did exist as a twelfth-century grammarian whose notes on Priscian survive. He will do as our starting-point.

*This chair lives in the High Master's study, and has been the High Master's chair since at least the time of Richard Roberts (1769–1814).*

*In 1509, the year which tradition keeps as the foundation of St Paul's School, Erasmus wrote his* Praise of Folly (Moriae Encomium), *dedicated to Thomas More. Here Folly sits as schoolmaster, armed with birch instead of bells.*

Medieval bishops were much too grand to teach in school themselves, though a good bishop trained promising young men in his household, as Archbibishop Theobald did Thomas Becket, who had, perhaps, earlier been to school at St Paul's. The teaching in the Cathedral was the business of the clergy who managed the Cathedral, namely the chapter – the dean and canons – and their numerous subordinates. About 1120 the Bishop of London granted Hugh the Schoolmaster and his successors the room in the corner of the tower which Durandus used to have. The tower was free-standing, at the east end of the Cathedral, very near the future site of Colet's school.

By the thirteenth century, if not earlier, there were two schools maintained by the Cathedral, a grammar school, governed, and perhaps at first taught, by the Chancellor, who was one of the canons, and a choir school, governed by the Almoner. It is the grammar school which was the ancestor of our St Paul's School, though the choirboys (eight or ten in number) seem to have gone in crocodile to the grammar school for some of their lessons, and may well have been sent on there to study full-time when their voices broke.

A grammar school, like a secondary school today, was the middle tier of a three-tiered educational system. Grammar meant Latin, not only what we would call Latin grammar, but fluency in the language, written and spoken, and some knowledge of its literature. Before beginning on it, the boys had to learn their ABC, and perhaps some literacy in English. The choirboys also learned music, of course,

*The west end of Cheapside in 1585. The upside-down gate leads into the Cathedral churchyard. St Paul's School was just off the picture, a few yards to the south.*

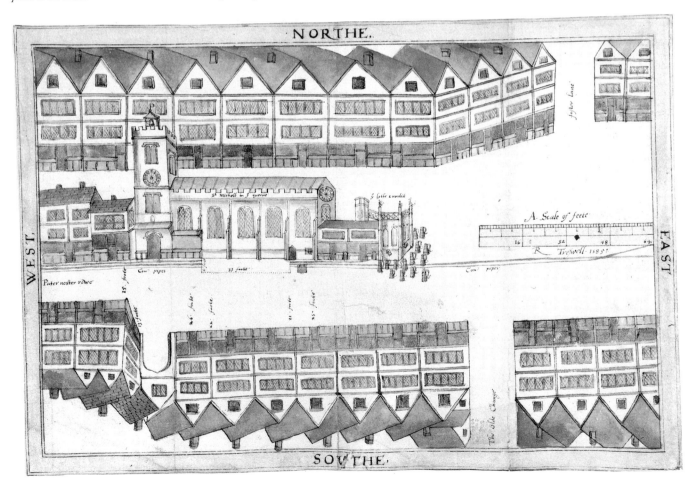

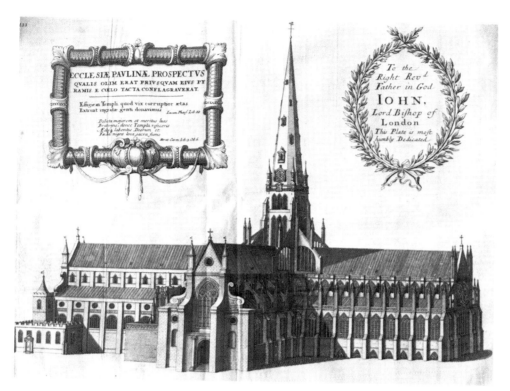

Old St Paul's Cathedral, before the
destruction of the steeple by fire in
1561, seen from the south. The
School was again just off the picture,
to the right.

and could probably sing the Latin services long before they could understand them:
but medieval schoolboys began their education very early on, and it was not
uncommon to be at the university at thirteen. Grammar was the first of the liberal
arts, the portico of learning; after the boys had got through it, they could go
on to higher things – which, for those who persevered academically, meant the
dialectic, Aristotelian logic, which dominated the great 'schools' or universities
of Paris and Oxford.

Although Chaucer may have attended either or both of the Cathedral schools,
they fell into obscurity in the century between his day and Colet's. One schoolmaster at Paul's made an unfunny political epigram about Richard III; another,
Elwin by name, among other works of piety, was a great disciplinarian, and St
Erkenwald saved a schoolboy from his rod. But, despite the Chancellor's legal
monopoly, St Paul's and the two other established London schools were unable
to prevent the growth of rival institutions.

It is hard to be sure whether the school was still functioning when Colet became
Dean about 1505. Its premises were tiny, and over some shops (*antiqua scola cum
quatuor shopis subtus*). The new school, built a few yards further north, gained possession of them, and seemingly took over the obligation to help educate the choirboys. Colet's pupils, contrary to his orders, continued the ancient and rowdy
debates with other schools; and 'as the master of the Grammar School ... has
always been a member of our body', the High Master continued, whether priest
or layman, to have a stall in the Cathedral choir. In 1512 Colet called the old
grammar school '*schola nullius plane momenti*' – obviously a school of no importance. He could clear it away and build anew.

A medieval schoolmaster at work.

# II

## 'THE SCHOOL OF JESUS . . .
A TROJAN HORSE'

*Thomas More*

### THE NEW FOUNDATION

*'In devices of this kind one actually aims at a certain degree of obscurity in order to exercise the guessing powers of those who look at them.' Erasmus (here portrayed in old age by Holbein in 1535) on Terminus.*

JOHN COLET (1467–1519) probably went to school in London himself, perhaps at St Anthony's, his own school's future rival. His father, Sir Henry Colet, was a Mercer with property in Buckinghamshire. John Colet may have been an undergraduate at Cambridge and, around 1493–6, continued his education by travelling in Italy and France. On his return he quickly acquired a reputation from his lectures at Oxford on St Paul, and soon also acquired valuable preferment in the Church, even before he was ordained priest in 1498. Although he attacked pluralism in his famous reforming sermon of 1512, he held canonries at York and Salisbury until his death, as well as, for a time, the rich vicarage of Stepney. He was Dean of St Paul's by 1505.

There are two portraits of Colet with a claim to be taken seriously as likenesses: the bust by Torrigiano and the drawing by Holbein. These two are one, the drawing being almost certainly taken from the bust, and not from life. In both Colet appears serene, grave, reflective; perhaps also rather severe. It is easy to see in the portraits confirmation of Erasmus's account of a man who had successfully conquered strong passions, and a host who would provide edifying conversation, but not a very large dinner.

Colet was a paradoxical man, and the problems about him interweave with the problems about his new school. Its degree of continuity with the medieval grammar school is an old, and rather barren, controversy. More important, and more complex, is to determine the place of Colet's school in the educational changes of his day. It certainly influenced other new and reformed schools. The statutes of Sherborne, Merchant Taylors', the King's School, Canterbury, and the Mercers' own school were among those that borrowed from St Paul's. We are sure that it was to teach the new learning, but much less sure how Colet understood that new learning. He was a reformer, but few would now see him as a Reformer: he was no Protestant before his time, though later Protestants tried to hijack him for their cause. He is something of a Janus figure – or, better, a Terminus, the boundary-mark which was the personal 'logo' of his friend Erasmus.

All ages face both ways, and it is dangerous to take it for granted that this was especially true of the period that has been labelled the Renaissance, or the end of the Middle Ages, or the beginning of modern history. This is a particular temptation for historians of St Paul's School, whose foundation looks an obviously Renaissance event. The date is another antiquarian's chestnut, and causes headaches when centenaries come round. The traditional year is 1509, but Colet was taking the first steps by 1508, and may not have admitted the first boys until 1512. Thus we can date the School either from the brave new years of that humanists' bright hope, King Henry VIII, or from the last days of the older historians' new monarch, Henry VII, who has recently begun to look so much more medieval. Still, even if C. S. Lewis's claim to have proved that the Renaissance never happened is treated with respect, those years were years of conscious innovation, and Colet was trying, in a rather traditional manner, to do something new.

*Below left: Torrigiano's bust of Colet was made for the monument in the Cathedral, probably from a death mask. The head of this cast, which was in the School for almost all its history, may be contemporary. In 1887 Mr Harris, the Art Master, removed seventeen coats of paint.*

*Below: Holbein's drawing of John Colet, now at Windsor Castle, is certainly posthumous and probably based on the bust. Perhaps drawn for Sir Thomas More in 1532 or 1533.*

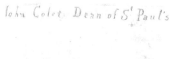

John Colet. Dean of St Paul's

Colet was a very rich man. The deanery of St Paul's and his other livings provided a handsome income, but he had also inherited a large fortune from his father, who was Lord Mayor of London, and whose twenty-one other children all died young. Colet lived frugally and gave everything he could to his School, gave so much that, in his last years, he found it hard to make ends meet. He thus succeeded in founding what was then the largest endowed school in England, more than twice as big as Eton (whose revised statutes provided for seventy boys) and with masters paid twice as well (in 1573, a former headmaster of Eton accepted the High Mastership of St Paul's). It may, too, have been a consciously lay institution, although an utterly Christian one. The obvious governors would have been the Cathedral chapter, but Colet was not on particularly good terms with them, perhaps because he had tried, and failed, to reform them. He chose instead his father's livery company, the Mercers; if Erasmus is to be believed, this is because 'though there was nothing certain in human affairs, he yet found the least corruption in' married laymen. The first High Master was also a layman, but this was not particularly unusual: though Eton, like its model, Winchester, was intended as a college of priests incorporating a school for training future priests, the usher there was forbidden to be in holy orders. Colet prayed that his boys should grow up to be great clerks: but he meant scholars, not clerics. He thought that there were too many priests anyhow, and that more meant worse.

Yet it would be as mistaken to secularize Colet and his intentions as to Protestantize them. He was a fervent, celibate and ascetic priest who urged on the boys of his School frequent confession and devotion to the Virgin Mary. He dedicated the School to her and to her son, Jesus, in His boyhood; it was sometimes called 'Jesus School' at first. He endowed a chantry in connection with his new School. The dignity of the priesthood, higher than that of any layman, even a king or an emperor, is central to his thinking. It is taken for granted when, in his Convocation Sermon of 1512, he urges reformation on the clergy. In his School, the Chaplain is to sing mass daily, though the boys are not to attend the whole mass, but only to kneel in their seats and pray when they hear the bell ring as the host is consecrated. Three times a day, too, they are to pray prostrate. When warned to do so, they are to take part in processions, two by two, saying (not singing) seven psalms and the litany. On Childermas (Innocents' Day) they are to go to St Paul's Cathedral and hear the boy bishop preach before High Mass. At first, apparently, there was no chapel in the School, though a chantry was attached to it, and no chaplain's name is known from Colet's day. Perhaps the boys went daily to the Cathedral, and were ministered to under Colet's own supervision. He certainly wrote prayers for his pupils, and a 'Cathechyzon', or summary of the Faith.

If the Chaplain was learned enough, he was to help with the teaching, 'if it shall seem convenient to the High Master, or else not'. The learning did not need to be very great: he was to teach elementary Latin grammar and religious knowledge. At the time of Colet's death, Erasmus describes the School as arranged in three divisions, with the Chapel as a fourth. They are separated by curtains. In the lowest division the Chaplain teaches the little boys; in the middle, the Surmaster teaches the middle-sized boys; in the third, the High Master teaches the big boys.

*Illustration to a manuscript of the gospels, made for Colet and now in Cambridge University Library. The figure on the right, perhaps intended to be Colet, was described by Sir Thomas Smith (1662) as 'having the beautifullest Face (in my opinion) that I ever beheld'.*

The boys sit on benches, raised in tiers; each class contains sixteen. If there were eight classes from the beginning, that would mean 128 boys. But it is hard to divide 128 boys on eight benches neatly between three masters, and anyhow, Colet ordained that there should be 153 boys. Erasmus's scheme is rather too pat.

It is worth pausing on the famous 153. A much more sensible number would have been 160, given eight forms and two regular masters, with the Chaplain's teaching either auxiliary or an afterthought. The allusion to the miraculous catch in the last chapter of St John's Gospel seems obvious, and since the nineteenth century Foundation Scholars have worn a fish on their watch-chains, or, more recently, in their button-holes. Neither Colet nor any other sixteenth-century writer actually makes the connexion, though the Mercers had made symbolic use of the miraculous catch in a mummery presented to the Lord Mayor about 1425. Lupton and McDonnell are doubtful about it. But there is no other likely explanation, and their reluctance to accept it probably reflects, if unconsciously, a wish to make Colet an acceptable Renaissance man, progressive and enlightened; a common-sensical, almost a Whiggish, liberal Christian. It is quite true that Colet strongly disliked the over-elaborate theology of the late medieval scholastics, with their verbal subtleties and endless layers of meaning. But it would be a mistake to suppose that he wished to replace this with a simple literal approach. His biblical thought, which concentrates on St Paul, is strongly ethical, but it is also strongly mystical: he was a real Renaissance man, not a Renaissance man as seen through later progressive spectacles. He had read, and may have met, the Florentine Platonists, Pico and Ficino: he believed that the universe was ordered hierarchically, that its order was numerically structured and that understanding was to be had by applying numerical keys, especially the key of threes: in short, he admired and used, above all other writings outside Scripture, the early sixth-century neo-Platonic Christian mystic, pseudo-Dionysius.

Colet believed this writer to have been the first-century Dionysius whom St Paul met in Athens, and so thought his works to be among the earliest Christian writings to exist, composed in the very shadow of the great apostle. He was rather old-fashioned in thinking this. It had been taken for granted for centuries, but had been attacked convincingly in his own lifetime by his own friend, Grocyn. Colet, who knew little or no Greek, was holding a line that he must have known to be defensive. That it mattered to him reveals a side of Colet very different from the straightforward Christian moralist, admirer of the lay and married state, and founder of a school based on these wholesome simplicities, who has been the patron of so much Pauline self-congratulation. Why then 153 fishes? Perhaps (a still fairly straightforward solution) because, it was thought, there were 153 species of fish in existence, corresponding to the command to preach the gospel to all nations, and St Paul's was to be a school for 'all nacions and countres indifferently'. But perhaps for more cabbalistic reasons: 153 is the triangular of the mystic number 17 'the sum of ten and seven, both symbols of perfection' – that is, a triangle of 153 dots with one dot at the top, two in the next row, and so on, has a base of 17. As soon as a boy entered the School he was to be taught the Ten Commandments, and in the Catechyzon, the seven sacraments; upon this basis his education would be built: 'By this waye thou shalte come to grace and to glory. Amen.'

In 1513 Henry VIII, about to go to war, interviewed Colet who had just preached in favour of peace. The Dean emerged in the royal favour: 'Let every man have his own doctor . . . this is the doctor for me.' This nineteenth-century drawing gives the King the girth and dress which he only acquired when Colet had long been dead.

*The High Master's country house at Stepney. On this site Dame Christian Colet, the Dean's mother, lived as a widow. She left the boys at St Paul's 2d. each in her will, on condition that they attend her funeral.*

*Part of the Agas map of London (after 1561 – the spire has gone from St Paul's Cathedral). The arrow points across Old Change to the approximate site of Colet's School.*

Perhaps. . . . There is pleasure to be derived from the idea that a school so closely associated in reputation with the dawn of a prosaic, Protestant, middle-class England should have at the heart of its foundation one of the wilder fancies of Christian platonism. But the idea may be only a fantastic fancy itself: in his later years, at any rate, Colet stressed Christian living more strongly than 'cabbalistic and Pythagorical' speculations. It is salutary to return to the Statutes, and find how prosaic he can be. After the boy bishop, and the sober litanies two by two, comes this necessary regulation:

> To theyr urin they shall goo thereby to a place appointed and a pore Childe of the scole shall se it conveyde a way fro tyme to tyme and have the avayle of the uryn. For other causis if nede be they shall goo to the water syde.

Colet's new School was 'elegantly built in stonework and established in the Eastern part' of the Cathedral churchyard near the site of the old Cathedral grammar school. Adjoining it were houses, perhaps half-timbered, for the High Master and Surmaster. No picture of the building survives, though a formalized glimpse of it can be caught from Ralph Agas's view of London towards the end of the sixteenth century. A plaque on what is now the wall of the Cathedral choir school marks the site. Colet purchased it from the chapter and the City. He also endowed the School with lands in London, Whitechapel, Buckinghamshire and elsewhere, with an annual income in 1579 of £166. He provided the High Master with a country house in Stepney.

The churchyard was not a sheltered close, but a crowded centre of business and social life, which spilled over, despite the efforts of the church authorities, into the Cathedral itself. In particular, through all the centuries of the School's life there, it was the home of printers and booksellers. The School's life was never insulated from the life of the City. Indeed, the Mercers' Company, who were to govern the School and administer its property, are the first of the great twelve City companies. For about a century after Colet's day they were still deeply involved in mercery, international trade in high-quality cloth. Real power in the Mercers' Company, and the real government of the School, belonged to the Court of Assistants, the Master, three wardens, past masters and Aldermen members, together with the Company's chief officer, the Clerk. The Surveyor Accountant, who was always a senior Mercer, had direct responsibility for the income from the Colet estate, and for expenditure on the school. Like the Master and Wardens, he held office for one year at a time, which may have helped some High Masters get away with a good deal. The Company's most recent historian considers that the Elizabethan Mercers were conscientious trustees, who deserved Colet's high opinion and their sweeping powers. These included unlimited right to alter the statutes, which they did, extensively, in their Amending Ordinances of 1602. They dealt personally with such questions as whether the High Master should be allowed to take in fee-paying boarders (no) or to sublet rooms in his house (no). Only one early High Master (Malim in 1578) was himself admitted a Mercer. Being for the most part plain (though often very wealthy) merchants, the Court of Assistants took to calling in an annual conclave of learned men to help them assess

John Milton, painted by Cornelius Jannsen in 1619, when Milton was ten and had probably been at St Paul's for two or three years. (© The Pierpont Morgan Library 1990.)

'Was't not enough the holy Church had been
Invaded in her Rites and Discipline?
Must her known Fundamentals be baptiz'd
In purging flames, and Pauls School chatechiz'd?
She that had long her tardy Pupills stripp'd
Is now herself with fiery Scorpions whipp'd.'
(John Crouch, Londinenses Lacrymae, 1666)

(Museum of London.)

the academic health of the School. By 1559, this had become known as Apposition.

'When I hear my Colet,' said Erasmus, 'I seem to be listening to Plato himself': but 'no more deadly or irrational scheme could have been propounded', wrote C. S. Lewis of the syllabus which Colet proposed for his School. Despite his reputation among the humanists, despite, or because of, his admiration for clean and chaste Latin, the authors he ordered Paulines to read were all (except for two moderns) Christian writers of late antiquity whom no classicist would dream of putting on a school curriculum nowadays. It is unlikely that Colet was disingenuously hiding his real plans out of fear of his conservative bishop; more likely that he was less friendly to the pagan classics than Erasmus would have us believe. For children at least, in Colet's view, it may have been not only 'specially' but exclusively 'Cristyn auctours' who constituted 'good literature' as opposed to the filthiness 'whiche the later blynde worlde brought in which more rather may be called blotterature' and which 'I utterly abannyshe and exclude out of this Scole'. Thomas More associated the School with Christian Reform rather than pagan Renaissance: 'I am not surprised', he wrote to Colet, 'that the school of Jesus excites the envy and anger of dissolutes and obdurates. These perverse people can only contemplate with fear the crowd of Christians who, like the Greeks from the Trojan horse, spring from that academy to destroy their ignorance and disorder.'

Whatever Colet's intentions, there is no doubt that the pagan classics, Greek as well as Latin, were soon being studied at St Paul's. The first High Master, Lily, exhorts the boys to read Virgil, Terence and Cicero, and almost certainly taught them Greek too. St Paul's may well have been the first English school where Greek

An elementary grammar for use in St Paul's School, published in 1515. This copy, now in the School Library, belonged to High Master Kynaston and seems to have cost him a guinea. It is entirely in Latin.

Paul's Walk:
'No place so sacred from such fops
    is barred,
Nor is Paul's church more safe
    than Paul's churchyard:
Nay fly to altars; there they'll
    talk you dead;
For fools rush in where angels
    fear to tread.'

(Alexander Pope)

17

was studied; it was controversial and exciting, as it opened the door to a critical study of Christian origins, not to mention large and little-known tracts of pagan literature. Under Freeman, the fourth High Master, Greek disappeared, but he taught the eighth form Caesar, Horace, Ovid and Cicero, and insisted on 'figures Troppes Elegancies Notable Sentences Adages and p.graphs'. Greek soon recovered, and Hebrew was added, probably under Malim, and certainly by the seventeenth century. By that time the School may have dropped all the ancient authors that Colet recommended, and some of his own works were said to have perished because of the carelessness of the boys. But Erasmus's *Colloquies* survived, and 'Lily's Grammar' lived and grew.

Erasmus, though he declined to teach at St Paul's himself, was prepared to try to recruit teachers and to write textbooks for the new School. The *Colloquies* are lively Latin conversations, intended to sweeten the first stages of using the language, the kind of 'pretty book' recommended by an early editor of the Grammar. The Grammar itself, really a composite work in which Colet, Lily, Erasmus and Ritwise (Lily's successor) all had a hand, was at first short and simple, for Colet wanted the boys to move on quickly from rules to real reading. English is used in expounding the accidence, but the syntax is all in Latin – a mistake, Milton was later to argue. By Milton's day, though, 'Lily's Grammar' had swollen vastly, been given a royal monopoly, and changed its name. As *A Short Introduction to Grammar* it was the only such work officially permitted in English schools into the eighteenth century. In 1758 it was stolen by Eton, and renamed *The Eton Latin Grammar*. It was still in use at St Paul's in the 1840s.

Peter Carew, one of the earliest known Paulines, 'neither loved the School nor cared for learning'. He later became a muleteer, an adventurer and a prisoner in the Tower of London. It is likely that there were others like him, though those whose names survive are naturally mostly those who successfully got through the system. Even Milton, its success story *par excellence*, thought far too long was spent on grammar – 'seven or eight years meerly in scraping together so much miserable Latine and Greek, as might be learnt otherwise easily and delightfully in one year'. By his day 'Lily's Grammar' had turned into such a burden as it had been written to remove.

For the most part, the early High Masters were not hidebound or narrow-minded men. Mulcaster and Gill (senior) were imaginative writers on education, and even Jones, the least successful, was called 'learned and modest' by Polydore Vergil. But their reforming educational programme was a severe one: however much Mulcaster and Gill may have admired the vernacular, there was, they knew, only one, painful, ascent to Parnassus.

On the shelves of the London Library 'education' and 'flagellation' are near neighbours. A distinguished schoolmaster was traditionally expected to be an energetic flogger, and several early High Masters beat with pre-Freudian gusto. Malim came from Eton with a reputation discussed years later by statesmen who had suffered under him. Harrison actually made one of his pupils praise the rod, which sifts 'out the good seeds of our wits and cleanses our mind from the rust of impiety and Idleness'. When Mulcaster was whipping a boy one day, 'his breeches being down', the High Master was taken by a 'merry conceit', and said: 'I ask the bannes

*Ecce Puer fructus, ad quos ludi ipse Magister,*
*Et Pater invitant, & bene notus Amor.*
*Sæpe ulta est raptos crudelis Betula malos,*
*Nunc ut devites verbera carpe Puer.*
*T.W.*

*In this illustration from* A Short Introduction to Grammar, *schoolboys are encouraged to climb the tree of knowledge:*
*'Often has the birch avenged the*
*plundered apple tree,*
*But now to escape thrashing you*
*must apple pickers be.'*

of Matrymony between this boy his buttockes . . . and Lady Birch.' The boy managed a smart reply – 'Master I forbid ye bannes . . . because all partyes are not agreed' – and escaped, though Mulcaster in his educational writings argued for inflexibility and instant execution. He was in many ways an advanced thinker, advocating mathematics, modern languages and football. But he believed the birch essential as 'a means of compelling obedience where numbers have to be taught together'. It was unsafe to take advantage of his regular nap during morning school.

Alexander Gill senior, the longest-reigning and one of the most successful of the early High Masters, was the most famous flogger of all, and was warned by the Governors for overdoing it. Gill beat an old Pauline called Triplett, who was rash enough to visit the School after telling tales about him at Oxford. Aubrey says that he beat a man caught pissing outside the School and suspected of breaking a window. Triplett had rude songs composed about Gill and sung outside the schoolhouse. They alleged that Gill used to beat more or less at random – a Frenchman for asking the way to the Cathedral, a maid-servant for spoiling the dinner, and a Welshman, apparently just for being Welsh.

> In Paul's church-yard in London
> There dwells a noble firker;
> Take heed you that pass
> Lest you taste of his lash,
> For I have found him a jerker.
> Still does he cry
> Take him up, take him up, Sir,
> Untruss with expedition.
> Oh the birchen tool
> That he winds i' th' school
> Frights worse than an inquisition.

*This woodcut of the master enthroned, with the birch conveniently to hand, illustrates the* Catechism *of Alexander Nowell, Dean of St Paul's and cousin and patron of High Master Harrison.*

Another such song has him beating his son, the future High Master, and already a graduate, in front of the Surmaster and the boys.

> Though thou hast payd thy fees
> For thy degrees:
> Yet I will make thy arse to sneeze.
> And now I doe begin
> To thresh it on thy skin
> For now my hand is in, is in.

In the 1960s, new masters at St Paul's were informed that 'any master may beat any boy at any time'. Most of them seldom or never did so, but boys could still be seen in the corridors bringing the cane from the Head Porter for their own chastisement. Today the cane is kept in the Archives, and occasionally displayed in a glass case; but no master nowadays has to spend all day, as sixteenth-century masters often did, with the same fifty boys of a very wide age-range, teaching them almost nothing but Latin, and requiring them to speak Latin even in their playtime.

19

# III

## 'THE MASTER OF THE GRAMMAR SCHOOL CANNOT BE TOO CAREFULLY SELECTED'

*Richard Mulcaster*

### 1509–1608

THE EARLY MASTERS AT ST PAUL'S were mostly youngish men. The Chaplains (or Under-ushers) were indeed often very young, just down from the university, and many of them only stayed a year or two. Between 1556 and 1571 there were at least ten. They often lodged in the High Master's house, were accordingly expected to be single and sometimes expressly forbidden to marry. In 1600 a house was built for the Chaplain at the east end of the Cathedral, but in 1620 the Privy Council ordered it to be pulled down as a blemish and a nuisance. (The school porter pulled it down and was allowed to keep the materials.) In 1575 the Under-usher, Robert Bradshaw, was dismissed as 'a brawler and quarreller and also somewhat suspect in religion and not fit to teach'. In 1577 his successor's demand for higher wages was answered by dismissal because he was unthrifty and 'spendeth his time without profitting the scollers'. In 1583 the 'Lowest Master' was again dismissed, because he caused quarrels between the High Master and Surmaster 'in carrying tales and reports from one to the other to set them at variance and deadly hate'. He was given four months' wages, 'in consideration of his poverty', but had to leave his room in the High Master's house within a week. Yet such was the struggle for jobs among young graduates that in 1575 'a young man wayted a moneth at Powles School hoping to have been placed in Bradshawe's room'.

A few years later, Richard Mulcaster, soon to become High Master, wrote of the danger of educating too many men, 'to have so many gasping for preferment, as no gulf hath store enough to suffice'.

There were fourteen Surmasters between 1509 and 1640. Of these, three were certainly and six probably in their twenties. John Medley, the first Old Pauline known to have taught at the School, was still a schoolboy in 1571 and Surmaster in 1578. Richard Smyth, also a Pauline, became Surmaster at twenty. Christopher Holden, appointed in 1561, was thirty. George Gill, at thirty-five, was elderly – by that age Smyth had been pensioned off for 'decay of his eyesight and impotency' – but then Gill was the High Master's brother. The age of the other three is unknown.

The High Masters were, of course, older. There were ten between 1509 and 1640. The only two whose ages are not known are Jones and Freeman, in office from 1532 to 1559, turbulent years for both School and nation. Jones had graduated more than twenty years before he became High Master; Freeman had served for five years as the first headmaster of Mercers' School. Of the other eight, four were in their forties, two in their thirties, Harrison was twenty-nine and Mulcaster was sixty-five when he was appointed in 1596, and he retired (to a London parish) at seventy-seven. Four of the ten were already experienced headmasters and one of these, Malim, after a short spell as headmaster of Eton, had been on diplomatic service in the Levant. Three others were promoted from the Surmastership, and Gill junior had been Under-usher. The average age at appointment works out at forty-one, rather young by modern standards, but not so young as to explain their numerous quarrels with the Governors and the other masters, and their sometimes violent behaviour.

The Mercers' government of the School was intimate and all-embracing. Mercers' Hall was a few hundred yards away: but the Apposing (at first appositely spelt 'opposing') Chamber, in which masters and boys were annually put through their paces, was in the School, over the High Master's rooms. From the first, Mercers sent their sons to St Paul's, and soon, since membership was largely hereditary, there were Mercer Old Paulines and Old Pauline Governors, among them such men of affairs as Sir Thomas Gresham and Baptist Hicks, Viscount Campden; but the Mercers' control was not free from challenge or insubordination. Masters could seek to sidestep it and outsiders to invade it. During the School's first century there were three major notes of disharmony: the religious controversies of the age, the poverty or avarice of the masters, and the unshakeable thirst of the great for patronage and of the small for employment. These can be illustrated by the strange and stormy careers of several early High Masters, four of the first ten of whom were dismissed, while two others narrowly escaped dismissal.

William Lily, the first High Master, was a grammarian of international reputation, one of the first Englishmen to be fluent in Greek as well as Latin, a close friend of Erasmus, godson of Grocyn and confidant of the Founder. Lily and Thomas More had lived together when they were both considering a vocation to the priesthood and even to that strictest of religious lives, the Carthusian. Both, however, had turned instead to marriage. Lily's pupils included John Clement, who married More's adopted daughter, Margaret, and probably John More,

*The arms of the Mercers' Company – 'A demi-virgin couped below the shoulders . . . her hair dishevelled' – have been prominent features of all the School buildings.*

*Elizabethan Cheapside. Mercers' Hall is the prominent building, bottom centre.*

21

VERA EFFIGIES

ætatis suæ 52·1520

*The only known portrait of the first*
*High Master, William Lily.*

More's youngest child. They also included several major statesmen: one of them, Sir Anthony Denny, Groom of the Stool, warned Henry VIII of his approaching death; a second, Lord Chancellor Southampton, weeping, announced the death to parliament; a third, Sir William Paget, Secretary of State, read the will.

Two of Lily's pupils held the Readership in Rhetoric founded by Wolsey at Corpus Christi College, Oxford, that centre of the new learning; a third, John Leland, has been called 'the founder of historical research in England'. Though the names of most of his pupils – indeed of the vast majority of early Paulines – are lost, there can be no doubting the éclat of the infant foundation or of the High Master. 'An honourable and most experienced man', Richard Pace called Lily in a letter to Colet published in 1517; the boys 'have an instructor whose life and morals have both stood the test of time'. The humanists liked to praise one another in florid hyperbole, but Lily's reputation was unassailable – and Colet himself lived through all but the last three years of his friend's High Mastership.

Colet had wished the Surmaster, if suitable, to succeed to the High Mastership, and when Lily retired in 1522, the Mercers duly appointed John Ritwise, who was not only Surmaster, but also Lily's son-in-law. Ritwise, then thirty-two, was the first of five early High Masters to have been at Eton and King's College, Cambridge. At first all went well: a year after his appointment, Ritwise was congratulated by the Governors; in June 1525 the school was overflowing. But that December, in 1526, and again in 1531, he was rebuked with increasing severity, and in November 1532 he was said to be 'ever worse and worse' and 'utterly expelled, amoved and put forth of the same rome of Scolemaistershippe'. He was given a pension, all the same, a lodging and £10 a year, nearly a third of his salary as High Master.

In what ways Ritwise dissatisfied the Mercers is not clear. He seems to have agreed with them to turn away boys beyond the statutory number and to prefer Londoners to others, yet in the year of his dismissal he was educating at least one non-Foundationer, George Frauncs, 'the King's Scholar', at Henry VIII's expense. McDonnell thought the Mercers may have objected to the dramatic performances, in Latin and French, that Ritwise and his boys performed before the King and the Cardinal: 'I suspect that his interest in playwriting was his undoing as a schoolmaster.' But perhaps he just grew idle or ill: he died six months after his dismissal.

The next two High Masterships have been called the Dark Ages of the School's history. No one pupil of Richard Jones (1532–49) can be named for certain. William Harrison, the Chronologer, later wrote that when he was one of 'the children of Pawles Scholl', he was made to buy the English Litany: but he may have been at the Cathedral choir school, where it would also have been needed. Three of the other possibles were sons of the Surmaster. The only certain pupil of Thomas Freeman (1549–59) appears to be Robert Laneham, who was, by his own account, Mercer, merchant adventurer, musician, drinker, 'clerk of the council chamber door and also Keeper of the Same'; he also went to the rival school, St Anthony's. It is possible that both Edmund Campion, the Jesuit martyr, and William Fulke, the Puritan controversialist who disputed with him in the Tower of London, were at St Paul's when they disputed as schoolboys in 1552. Nothing is even known of Freeman's origin or education.

Undeterred by the failure of Ritwise, the Mercers raised up Jones from the Surmastership. In 1534, they ordered him not to allow the boys, contrary to Colet's Statutes, to go debating against boys from other London schools. In 1535, 1536 and 1537 they reminded him and the Surmaster only to use the books authorized by Colet and others that conformed to the King's pleasure and the laws of the Church. In 1542, not for the first time, High Master and Surmaster were warned, on pain of immediate dismissal, 'to amend in plying of the scolers to their learning'. They were warned again in 1543 and 1544. In 1545 Jones was given a last chance; in 1546 they agreed to keep him for another year; in 1547 he was to be removed if he failed an examination in Latin and Greek by 'good, sadde, charytable and dyscryte learned men'. This he passed satisfactorily, and, although in December 1548 the Mercers noted that there were 'none amendment founde on Jones behalfe as yet', he died, still High Master, on 5 October 1549.

Whereas Jones gave such cause for complaint that his death in office amounts to an outstanding survival, there were, apparently, no complaints at all about Freeman until December 1558. At an assembly in that month he and the Surmaster

Above: *Preaching at Paul's Cross, a covered pulpit in the Cathedral churchyard – 'the Times newspaper of the Middle Ages'.*

Above right: *James I attending a sermon in state, 1620. Here Elizabeth I had reduced Dean Nowell to tears. Paul's Cross and High Master Gill (junior) were both victims of the Puritan fury of the 1640s.*

'were found fault with as the schollers answered not as they have done in times past'. He was made to answer a series of questions on his method of teaching, and grilled, at Apposition, by a formidable group of learned divines, who watched him teach and sent him away to write a Latin essay on whether precept or example is more important. They did not think his Latin satisfactory, and a fortnight later asked him to compete with John Cook, headmaster of Sherborne, in writing verse or prose. When Freeman, goaded beyond endurance, refused the test, they asked him if he was learned in Greek. No, he replied, as had been well known when he was appointed. He was dismissed, and Cook, who had done his exercise in Greek as well as Latin, was installed in his place.

These two stormy High Masterships coincide almost exactly with the stormiest years of the English Reformation. Within a year of Jones's appointment Cranmer became Archbishop of Canterbury, Henry VIII married Anne Boleyn and parliament began the legislation that severed the link with Rome. Through all the changes that followed up to the early days of the next reign, Jones held his place (as did, on a larger and more dangerous stage, at least four Pauline privy councillors). Freeman survived the most rapid and bewildering changes under Edward VI and Mary – in 1554 one preacher at Paul's Cross had to flee into the School to escape being lynched – but within a year of the accession of Elizabeth I, Anne Boleyn's daughter, and while parliament was restoring the Reformation settlement, Freeman was dismissed.

Indeed, it is possible to be more precise. A month after Queen Mary's death, the Mercers expressed dissatisfaction with the High Master. Of the six learned men they invited to examine him in April, five (Cox, Horne, Whitehead, Jewel and Aylmer) were among the nine Protestant theologians who, that same April, had been engaged in an official debate against Marian bishops in Westminster Abbey. The purpose was not to give the bishops a chance to win, but to give them the appearance of a fair hearing. Poor Freeman must have known what to expect. After dinner it was decided that he should be given notice at midsummer: it was on Midsummer Day (24 June) that it became an offence to use any other church services than those authorized in the restored Protestant *Book of Common Prayer*, though the Latin mass had in fact been abandoned as early as 11 June in the last London church to keep it – St Paul's Cathedral. The image of Jesus in the School, however, which had been restored in Mary's reign, was not removed again until 1561–2.

It is impossible to doubt that the real reason for Freeman's dismissal was religious, though nothing appears to have been said about religion throughout the process. What is surprising is that such imposing theological heavies, who included the future bishops of London, Winchester, Ely and Salisbury, and who were deeply involved in the vital religious legislation in parliament, should have thought it worth spending time over crushing a schoolmaster. From this distance, they look like rhinoceroses presiding at a kangaroo court, though they probably felt that Freeman's ignorance of Greek was just what was to be expected of a religious obscurantist. Besides, they needed to get their hands on the future quickly: they did not know how long their power would last.

It is strange that James Jacob, the Surmaster, did not share the High Master's fate, though as he had served the School for nearly thirty years and died the following January, charity may have combined with calculation in staying the Mercers' hand. Jacob was, or had been, very deeply entrenched in St Paul's. His wife, Dionysia (christened, no doubt, for Colet's favourite author) was daughter of the first High Master, and widow of the second. She was a learned lady, like Thomas More's daughters, and may well have written *Dido*, the Latin tragedy performed by the School in 1528. Her brother, George Lily, was chaplain to Cardinal Pole, and prebendary of St Paul's. He died in 1559. Her nephew, John Lyly (*sic*), the euphuist, may have been vice-master of the choir school in the 1580s. Dionysia was at the heart of what looks rather like a dynasty.

Perhaps she had protected Jones as well. Her first husband had made him Surmaster; he had made her second husband Surmaster. But Jones, like Freeman, was probably, whatever his failings as a schoolmaster, valuable as a moderate and pliable conservative. Despite their frequent complaints about him, the Mercers retained him in the face of strong hints from high places: in 1544 and again in 1546 Queen Catherine Parr made recommendations for the High Mastership (which was not vacant). Later in 1546 Archibishop Cranmer suggested a third candidate. All three were Protestants. The Mercers clearly didn't like Jones, but they hung on to him, for fear of finding something worse.

Perhaps the interest of the Queen and the Archbishop and the six divines in the High Mastership reflects the importance of St Paul's in the mid-sixteenth century. Not that any post was too small for the attention of patrons or any school for the attention of reformers. It is probable that the Mercers' first reminder to Jones about teaching from the right books in 1535 was prompted by royal orders to schoolmasters issued by Thomas Cromwell that year.

*This medieval sketch of St Paul's Cathedral accompanies an account of the foundation of London by Brutus the Trojan. As for such stories, writes the learned Old Pauline antiquary William Camden (in his Britannia, English trans. 1610), 'I leave them to those that are inclin'd to admire them.'*

The involvement of the great continued. Although Colet had been on bad terms with his bishop and had been careful to exclude the Cathedral chapter from the government of the School, going so far as to petition the Pope to keep out the chancellor of the Cathedral, successive bishops of London, and deans and chapters, concerned themselves with it more or less effectually. Bishop Fitzjames, who had tried to prosecute Colet for heresy, may have attacked the School as a 'House of Idolatry ... because the Poets are read there'. Very soon after Colet's death, the chapter tried unsuccessfully to get rent from the School. The Elizabethan bishops Sandys, Grindal, Whitgift and Aylmer took a close interest. Grindal was one of the Apposers in 1569 and 1570. Sandys was closely involved in the appointment of a High Master in 1573 (though the successful candidate, William Malim, also enjoyed the more important patronage of the Earl of Leicester). In 1583 the Governors and Apposers went to dinner 'at Mr. Bishopp's House'.

More interested and influential than any bishop in the School's affairs was Alexander Nowell, Dean of St Paul's from 1561 to 1601. He was an educational pundit, an ex-headmaster (Westminster) and reviser of school rules (Tonbridge). He was also a strong if moderate Puritan, who though memorably put down by Elizabeth I – 'to your text, Mr. Dean; to your text! leave that' – was the powerful centre of a web of like-minded friends and relations. One relation was John Harrison, whose appointment as Surmaster in 1580 and as High Master in 1581 he may well have managed. Another was John Hammond, who was the only other member besides Nowell of an official commission to decide whether the Governors were justified in trying to dismiss Harrison in 1586. A third was William Whitaker, whom Nowell had had educated at St Paul's to save him from his parents' 'popish superstitions', and whose Greek translation of Nowell's own catechism Harrison was ordered to teach his pupils.

Harrison had made himself objectionable to the Governors by 'his little continuance in the school, the small number of his scholars and the weakness of those he hath', as well as by 'meddling with the lands and rents' and 'slandering of the company'. Soon after his appointment, he had 'violently expelled and put out of the scole the Surmaster and under usher and commanded them openly in the scole not to teach there nor the boies to obey them'. He was always asking for more pay. By 1596 the number of boys had sunk to fifty-two.

He was, however, extremely difficult to dislodge. Among those who backed him at one time or another were the Earls of Lincoln, Leicester, Warwick and Essex, Archbishop Whitgift and Sir Francis Walsingham. But Dean Nowell's backing was what really mattered: it was in 1596, when Nowell, then about ninety, did not attend Apposition, that Harrison was at last dismissed. Even then, he went down fighting: he would not send any boys to be examined; he would not get out of the High Master's chair; he said that the dean and chapter, not the Mercers, had the right to appoint the Apposers, and that the Mercers had illicitly removed the authentic Statutes from the School, substituting a 'maimed' and altered version 'mingled with their own devices'. He had to be ejected, eventually, by the Sheriff's Officers. (He lived on for years. In 1609 he successfully touched a former pupil, Lionel Cranfield, later Lord Treasurer, for £100.)

After the Apposition Dinners in 1584 and 1586, Harrison's pupils regaled the

Governors with dramatic dialogues written by the High Master. These were elaborately allegorical, each having eight characters, to represent the eight forms, and no action. They hinted, none too subtly, at Harrison's poverty: 'What is my Mr's living so little and yet doth he take so many paynes.' They also urged the Governors to provide exhibitions to help Paulines through the university, for want of which, Harrison claimed, boys were being removed to other schools. The Company had in fact endowed two such exhibitions in 1564, and by 1583 there were ten. (They preferred them to go to Mercers' sons if possible.) The dialogues may owe their ornate complexities to Lyly, the Euphuist: their simpler moments come from real schoolboy life:

My maister durst not beate you know whom bycause he is a mercer's son.

I will tell my mother of him and I will come no more to schole rather than I should be beaten.

He shall have my voyce to take more libertye and lesse paynes if he woulde but give us leave to play oftener than we doe.

But the High Master was not supposed to give them leave to play. A 'Remedy' is the Pauline word for a holiday, because it was Colet's word; he wrote: 'I will . . . that they shall have no remedyes.' 'If the maister granteth any remedyes he shall forfeit xls totiens quotiens [40s. for every one] excepte the Kyng, or an Arch-bisshopp, or a Bishop present in his own person in the Scole desire it.' Colet reckoned that Sundays and Holy days gave them, in any case, 153 days off; by the end of the century they had fewer saints' days, but their Thursday afternoons were free. Their games in the churchyard broke windows and disrupted the Cathedral services. Colet had disapproved of out-of-school activities, except for liturgical

*Monuments of Dean Nowell (far left) and Dean Colet (left) in old St Paul's Cathedral. In 1809 the headless torso of one bust was found in the vaults of the Cathedral. It was identified as Nowell, but was almost certainly Colet. It has since disappeared.*

ones, like the boy bishop's sermon. (On Innocents' Day it was traditional for choir-boys to choose one of their number to act the bishop's part for a day. Erasmus wrote a sermon about the boy Jesus which may have been intended for a boy bishop to preach.) There was to be 'no cockfightinge, nor rydinge about of victorye, nor disputing at Saint Bartilmewe, which is but foolish babling, and losse of time'.

These disputings went back to the twelfth century. They were debates between London schools, conducted in the old logic-chopping manner which Colet so disliked, and they often ended in violence, satchels full of books (if not of bricks) being used as weapons. 'Fellowes with greate sachells challenged us all to a solemn disputacon if we durst for the silver penne', one of Harrison's pupils maintained; and because the Paulines refused, they were taunted with:

> *Plus, plus, plurimus*
> *Semper tu es asinus.*

But Paulines, who were called 'Paul's Pigeons' by their opponents, after the flocks of pigeons 'bred in Paules Church' sometimes did take part, despite the Statutes, and one came second in the contest for the silver pen in 1555.

They also took part in the pageantry and drama of Tudor London. They delivered Latin addresses at coronation processions (which then used to set out from the Tower of London), they gave a pageant at Anne Boleyn's wedding in 1533, and in 1554 'a skoller of Paule's School decked up in cloth of gold' presented Philip II of Spain, then King Consort of England, with a 'fayre book which he receyved verye gentle'. The 'Children of Paul's', who were among the most successful of the boy actors of Elizabeth's reign, were from the choir school rather than Colet's School; but the choirboys were sometimes sent across to the main School to learn their Latin grammar and vice versa, 'for that learned Mr. Lillie knew full well that knowledge in music was a help and a furtherance to all arts'; so that the two schools were not wholly distinct.

The Mercers were not very happy about public performances, but they brought the masters to the attention of the great, and two Elizabethan High Masters, Malim and Mulcaster, had been much involved in drama at their previous schools. Marston's *What You Will* (c. 1601) has a schoolroom scene that may be based on St Paul's under Mulcaster, and Beaumont and Fletcher, in *The Knight of the Burning Pestle*, which flopped in 1610 or thereabouts, has a citizen's wife admiring a boy actor: 'Sirrah, didst thou ever see a prettier child? how it behaves itself, I warrant ye! and speaks and looks, and perks up the head! I pray you, brother, with your favour, were you never one of Master Moncaster's scholars?' In the seventeenth century, schoolboy drama wasted away, under religious disapproval and adult competition; but as late as 1627 Thomas Newton edited Terence's comedies *Andria* and *The Eunuch* 'for schollers private action in their schooles' and dedicated them 'to the schollers of Paules Schole', wishing them 'increase in grace and learning'.

Opposite: *After his removal, High Master Harrison retired to Norfolk, where he took Holy Orders, collected ancient coins, and became a locally notable eccentric.*

# IV

## 'THE PIGEONS OF PAUL'S FLUTTERED HIGHER THAN EVER'

*David Masson*, Life of John Milton

### 1608–1713

The preacher, who had been at St Paul's under Langley, describes him as 'not only an excellent Linguist and Grammarian, Historian Cosmographer, Artist, but a most judicious Divine, and a great Antiquary in the most memorable things of this Nation'.

THOUGH PUNCTUATED BY war and revolution, dispersal by plague and destruction by fire, the School's history during the seventeenth century is marked by increasing stability, growth and reputation. Three High Masters died in office, and were honourably buried in the ante-chapel of Mercers' Hall. One of these had served for twenty-seven years. A fourth, after twenty-five years as High Master, went on to be Dean of York. None of the great political disturbances of the century saw any significant break in the School's affairs. Recovery after the Great Fire was rapid and impressive. Competitors for the High Mastership, when vacant, were numerous and often distinguished. The School seems to have been full or overflowing, and the number both of boys of distinguished parentage and of Paulines with distinguished careers was as great, in proportion to the size of the School, as at any time in its history.

With one notable exception, seventeenth-century High Masters enjoyed much better relations with the Mercers than had been usual. This was doubtless one reason for the School's improving fortunes. Why relations got better is harder to say. Complaints about pay became rarer in the records, although the High Master's salary had risen from £34 3s. 4d. in 1512 to £109 6s. 8d. in 1592, a far higher rate of increase than in the following century and a half: it reached £169 6s. 8d. in

1700 and remained at that level until 1749, though it was supplemented by a regular and increasing annual bonus. But then the great inflation of the sixteenth century came to an end around 1650: also, the Governors tacitly abandoned the struggle to prevent the High Masters from admitting fee-paying pupils, including boarders, though they went on trying to stop them from letting rooms and accepting (or even demanding) tips from the boys or their families. Mulcaster fell seriously into the Mercers' debt, and they had to use his financial embarrassment to get him to vacate the High Master's house, when he retired in 1608. But when High Master Langley was dying in 1657 he left bequests to the Mercers, to buy plate and memorial rings.

More important still in the School's rising fortunes were the awards to help Paulines through the universities, though the Governors had more than once to forbid the practice of sending a boy to the School for a few months only, to entitle him to receive one of these exhibitions. They were increased from twelve to fifteen in 1619. The will of Viscount Campden (d. 1629) provided two more annually at Trinity College, Cambridge, and there were other bequests from Mrs Robinson and Lady North. They were almost essential to ambitious young men without means, for whom the Church with its exclusively graduate élite was almost the only ladder of success.

But not all Paulines were poor. Nor is St Paul's among the schools which, founded for the poor, have been filched by the rich. Or at least, though tuition was to be free, the Statutes do not say (though Stow, in his 1598 *Survey of London*, does) that it is for poor children: only, the 4*d*., payable by each child on his first admission, was to go to 'the poor Scoler that swepeth the Scole'. It is hard to see why Lord Brougham, the nineteenth-century reformer, thought that St Paul's was founded 'for the rich alone', even though the boys did have to bring expensive

*The Chapel of Mercers' Hall, as rebuilt in 1681. The Chaplain was sometimes one of the masters of St Paul's. The Chapel, with the rest of Mercers' Hall, was destroyed by an air-raid in 1941.*

*Halley's mural quadrant, which was installed at Greenwich in 1725, when he was Astronomer Royal. Halley's scientific interests were probably encouraged at St Paul's. While still a boy there, in 1672, he is said to have measured the variation of the magnetic compass.*

Opposite, top left: *This enormous portrait of High Master Roberts was presented to the School by Gildon Manton, who had entered it in 1806, aged sixteen.*

Opposite, top right: *This equestrian portrait of the 1st Duke of Marlborough, by Van Hughtenburg, hangs in the High Master's study. In 1725 a schoolfellow claimed that Marlborough learned the art of war by reading Vegetius in the School Library.*

Opposite below: *St Paul's School: 'The centre is adorned with rustic, and on the top is a well proportioned pediment, on which is displayed a shield with the arms of the founder, on the apex is a figure designed to represent learning.' (H. Chamberlain, Survey of London, 1770.)*

wax candles (a rule laid down by Colet, and still enforced in the 1820s); but some of the first Paulines had well-to-do parents. We have too few sixteenth-century names to make any useful analysis of Paulines' social backgrounds. In the seventeenth century the list is weighted by the large number of exhibitioners, who were, or were supposed to be, in need of financial help. None the less, Langley (High Master 1640–57) attracted a fair number of baronets and gentry, especially families which took the parliamentarian side in the Civil War. Cromleholme (1657–72) does not seem to have been so successful socially (though he educated Marlborough ('whipt at St Paul's School for not reading his Book') and, briefly, Judge Jeffreys ('occasionally flogged for idleness and insolence'); but under Gale (1672–97) and for a short time after him, Paulines included a few members of such great families as the Montagus, Stanleys, Mordaunts, Comptons and Osbornes, as well as the usual sons of clergymen, booksellers, Mercers, lawyers, drapers and (already a widely resorted-to coverall) gentlemen. The astronomer, Edmond Halley, who was Captain of the School, was the son of a soap boiler of good family.

The great also continued to meddle in appointments at the School. The Gill family was of obscure origin; but its connexion with St Paul's began with the unsuccessful attempt of the elder Gill, backed by the Earl of Northampton, on the Surmastership, and ended with the unsuccessful attempt of the younger Gill, backed by the Archbishop of Canterbury, to escape dismissal. Northampton was the friend and patron of the Old Pauline Lionel Cranfield, later Earl of Middlesex and Lord Treasurer, who had financial and political links with another Old Pauline, Baptist Hicks, Viscount Campden. Hicks's influence helped get Alexander Gill senior the High Mastership in 1608. A friend of Cranfield's, the Earl of Dorset (whose son later married Cranfield's daughter), got Gill's son out of serious trouble in 1628. Gill junior had been attacking Cranfield's bitter enemy, Buckingham, and later wrote verses in praise of Hicks's granddaughter, Penelope Noel. Cranfield lived long enough to ensure that his son's tutor succeeded the younger Gill in 1640.

The Gills were considerable nepotists: when one son was dismissed as Underusher, Gill senior promptly replaced him with the other; the elder son, who succeeded his father as High Master in 1635, promoted his brother to the Surmastership in 1637. But the two Alexander Gills were also remarkable men. The elder, though a Hebraist, as well as a 'noted Latinist, critic and divine', was a lover of English literature and blamed Chaucer (in Latin) for corrupting the language with Latinisms. His comparison of a contemporary poet, George Wither, to Juvenal aroused the contempt of Ben Jonson: Gill was his 'schoolmaster' who 'painted Time whipt, for terror to the Infantery'. His defence of orthodox Christianity (in English) may have won him the good offices of Archbishop Laud. This he badly needed, owing to the behaviour of his still more remarkable son.

Alexander Gill the younger was 'accounted one of the best Latin poets in the nation'. He was also violently indiscreet. It did not matter that he wrote abusive verses on Ben Jonson, to avenge his father: everybody quarrelled with Ben, who gave as good as he got. But, when his duties at school permitted, young Gill used to run down to Oxford and have a few drinks with his cronies. One such session began on a Monday morning in the summer. It was a day or two after the murder

ST PAVL'S SCHOOL.
Repaired and Beautified 1785 by the Worshipful Company of MERCERS
GOVERNORS
GYBBELSTON ROLFE Esq MASTER          PEREGRINE CUST Esq SURVIVOR WARDEN.

Above: *The arms of (from left to right) the Gill family, of High Master Langley and of Samuel Pepys, from a collection of manuscript paintings of Pauline coats of arms, probably made in preparation for the armorial glass which decorated the Great Hall at West Kensington.*

Left: *While at St Paul's, G. K. Chesterton's ambition was to be an artist. The Book of Fly, a collection of drawings in chalk of literary and legendary cats, was made for his first secretary, and given by her to a nephew who was at St Paul's in the Second World War. It is now in the School Library. (Reproduced by courtesy of John Allport.)*

of the Duke of Buckingham, and political excitement, as much as wine, overcame Gill completely. He made some broad hints about James I's private life, expressed himself sure that James and the Duke of Buckingham were together in hell, proposed a health to the assassin and remarked that King Charles I would be better fit to manage a Cheapside shop than to govern a kingdom. Unfortunately, one of his cronies was godson to Laud, the new Bishop of London, and grassed to his godfather. Laud had been Buckingham's chaplain and close friend. Gill was arrested in the schoolhouse, in front of the boys, taken to the Star Chamber and sentenced to lose his orders, his degree and both his ears, as well as to pay an enormous fine.

All he in fact lost was his Under-ushership; and within a year or two his father was employing him in the School as a supernumerary. Laud pitied, and perhaps admired the theology of, old Mr Gill, who begged for his son on his knees; he may not have been too tender to his old patron's memory either. Middlesex had been disgraced through Buckingham's agency; he was forbidden the court, but his friend Dorset was a rising star. By 1632 Gill junior was writing respectful verses to Charles and Laud. By 1635 he was High Master, and by 1637 Doctor of Divinity. More creditable to him than either was the admiration and lasting friendship of John Milton.

Milton may have entered St Paul's School as early as 1615, when he was seven. Aubrey says that when a schoolboy he sat up working till twelve or one o'clock at night, and wrote precocious verses. McDonnell cites among these the single line, shown up on his slate, on the miracle at Cana:

> The conscious water saw its God and blushed.

The slate, and the use of English rather than Latin, would be unlikely except in a junior form. Though the story seems to lack early authority, Milton certainly turned psalms into English verses while at St Paul's, and Christopher Hill sees in some of the renderings the radical influence of Gill the younger. A. N. Wilson, on the other hand, emphasizes Gill the elder's enthusiasm for spelling reform as the main Pauline influence on Milton, together with his decision to go to Cambridge (oddly, since Gill was an Oxford man). It is doubtful, too, whether his hard studies really cost him his eyes. Others have detected echoes of Prudentius, Lactantius and Baptista Mantuanus (all on Colet's reading list); but then Milton was a literary omnivore anyhow. By his own account he preferred reading and imitating 'the smooth Eligiack Poets' to any other form of recreation. As he wrote long afterwards:

> When I was yet a child, no childish play
> To me was pleasing, all my mind was set
> Serious to learn and know, and thence to do
> What might be publick good.

A severe enough schoolboy, if the literary self-portrait is to be trusted. But the young Milton, even if austere, was not yet a Puritan in Laud's sense, an enemy of the Church establishment. When the High Church Bishop Andrewes died in 1626, Milton, who had recently left St Paul's, had a literary vision of the old bishop in heaven, wearing a mitre and golden sandals. And in *Il Penseroso* (?1631) he recalls the worship of St Paul's Cathedral in language that would have warmed the heart of Laud, who had recently obtained an order in Council to prevent children playing there or idlers disturbing divine service.

Milton and the younger Gill corresponded for some years. They exchanged verses, and Milton praised Gill, whose conversation he compared favourably with what was to be had at Cambridge, both as a poet and as a 'very candid critic'. To Gill, he admitted that his Greek had got rusty since he left St Paul's. But while Milton was turning his back on the Laudian establishment, Gill was rebuilding his bridges to it, to good effect. He had got in his application for the High Mastership the day after his father died: but his success, by his own later account, was caused by the 'grace and favour' of the King.

It is not surprising that Gill's High Mastership was short, given that he was eighteen days absent without leave, that he seized the Poor Scholar by the jaw and kicked him up and down the School, and that the Master, Surveyors and other 'auntients' of the Mercers, found him drunk in the schoolhouse. But there is more to it than that. Gill was accused of all this in February and March 1639. The Governors only finally got rid of him two years later; even then they gave him £50 to leave and a pension of £25 a year. Meanwhile, in a petition to the King, Gill had accused them of misuse of the School's funds, and it is true that in 1640 the Mercers borrowed £1050 from the School's account to help them meet the heavy financial demands of the Crown and that they had borrowed smaller sums earlier. Gill's fortunes were closely linked to his patrons Laud and Windebank (the Secretary of State). Laud quarrelled with the Mercers over clerical patronage, and challenged their authority over St Paul's School. Gill supported him in this: he removed the Surveyors' coats of arms from his dining-room and told the Mercers they had no more right to turn him out than he had to turn them out. In February 1640, just after the arrival of Laud's ally Strafford from Ireland, the Mercers reluctantly gave Gill another six months' grace. Gill replied: 'I doe reject your warning.' In December Laud was arrested and Windebank fled the country; early in January 1641 Gill finally resigned. In September 1642 parliament's armies marched out of London to make war on the King; in October 1642 Gill was accused of an anonymous pamphlet attack on a Mercer (perhaps an indecent poem about Alderman Ashwick's cowardice), and his pension was stopped.

His successor, John Langley, had the recommendation of being an enemy of Laud. Laud, when Dean of Gloucester, had had him dismissed from the cathedral school there, which was presumably why he became a tutor in Lord Middlesex's household and thus eventually got the High Mastership. This is curious, though, since Middlesex was a High-Churchman and consulted Laud about the ritual in the chapel of his country house near Gloucester, whereas Langley accused Laud, at his trial in 1644, of High Church ritual goings-on in Gloucester Cathedral. Laud's interference with the Mercers' government of the School was brought up against him, too. A little war for control of St Paul's School had ended just as the great Civil War was beginning.

Samuel Pepys recalled in his diary that he was a great Roundhead when he was a boy and that he had said at school, on the day of King Charles's execution, that if he were to preach on him, his text would be 'the memory of the wicked shall rot'. On that same day another Pauline, Samuel Woodforde (great-grandfather of another famous diarist), went home from school to find his grand-father in tears – and retained his hatred of the regicides for the rest of his life. The Civil War cut clean across families and friendships – and schools. In 1648 the Old Pauline sub-dean of Wadham College, Oxford, William Thomas, was ejected as a royalist. In 1660 the Old Pauline President of St John's College, Oxford, Thankful Owen, was ejected as a Puritan.

As might be expected, though, identifiable Paulines of Roundhead background or inclination are more numerous than known Cavaliers. Langley was of high repute in the world of clerical Puritanism and his High Mastership sailed placidly through some of the most troubled years of English history, even if the School, like the other inhabitants of the churchyard in 1651, was disturbed by soldiers playing nine-pins and shouting at the passers-by. 'An excellent Linguist, and Gram-marian, Historian, Cosmographer, Artist', he could speak on any learned subject, and 'struck a mighty Respect and Fear in his Scholars, which, however, wore off after they were a little us'd to him.' His wish to be buried at the School door was not carried out; but he was probably fortunate to die when he did, at the height of his reputation, a year before the death of Cromwell. The boys of the school attended his funeral, wearing white gloves.

The earliest edition of the School's Latin prayers in the Library dates from 1644. It includes the conventional prayer for the king which asks 'that we his subjects, duly considering that he has his authority from thee, should faithfully submit our-selves to him'. It must have sounded odd. Times change. Pepys's politics changed; but his interest in his old School did not. He has been called the first Old Boy, and he was among the Old Paulines who, probably in 1661, began to gather to

These Engins, (which are ___ ___ the best) to quinch great Fires, are

JOHN KEELING Fecit

*Such engines were not very effective. On 5 September 1666 Pepys 'passed through Cheapside and Newgate market, all burned', and picked up a piece of glass from Mercers' Chapel 'so melted and buckled with the heat of the fire, like parchment'.*

hear a sermon and eat a dinner on the feast of the Conversion of St Paul; this was just called 'the Feast' by later Paulines. His visits to Apposition are the first indication of its being open to the public: in 1698 admission was confined to ticket-holders because of 'great Disorders' caused by boys and strangers. In 1660 he helped his younger brother prepare a Greek speech for the occasion 'though I believe he himself was as well able to do it as myself'. In 1663, as old boys do, he found that the standard had declined since his day: 'only in Geography they did pretty well'. He was something of a crony of High Master Cromleholme, Langley's nominee as his successor, though he thought him 'a ridiculous pedagogue ... though a learned man', and criticized him, from a glass house, for drinking too much.

On 7 September 1666, Pepys got up early and went to look at the effects of the Great Fire: 'all the towne burned, and a miserable sight of Paul's Church, with all the roofs fallen, and the body of the quire fallen into St. Faith's: Paul's school also.' The destruction was almost total. Only the sculpted head of Colet survived, and, astonishingly, perhaps some wooden panelling. The head remained in the School, its unique icon, through all vicissitudes, until 1969 when it was lent first to Rotterdam for the five hundredth anniversary of Erasmus's birth, and then to the Victoria and Albert Museum. The High Master lost his own library, thought by a contemporary to be the best private library in London; the loss was said to have shortened his life. The School, which had been closed for eight months in 1665 because of the plague, now dispersed, perhaps completely, until 1671. Cromleholme, whose wages were reduced for the time being to the £34 3s. 4d. laid down by Colet, opened a school in Wandsworth, which some boys from St Paul's may have attended.

It is much to the Mercers' credit that the School was rebuilt as soon as it was. They had themselves lost all their buildings, and were badly hit financially by

*'It made me weep to see it. The churches, houses and all on fire, and flaming at once, and a horrid noise the flames made, and the cracking of houses at their ruine.' (Pepys)*

*Invitation to the Feast, 1754, showing the rebuilt School after the removal of the louvre. The central figure symbolizes learning with, on either side, ornamental urns and the Mercers' demi-virgin. The design has been attributed (improbably) to Wren, and (rather less improbably) to Inigo Jones. The dinner began at 2 p.m. and cost 5s.*

loss of rent and of fines from lessees, and from lack of fire insurance. Mercers' Hall was not completely rebuilt until five years after the School reopened. It was fortunate that the Colet estate's property was little touched by the fire; even so, it had to borrow from the Company. The Mercers also fought off a scheme to widen the street which would have left the School with no site, and they even succeeded in acquiring additional space on which to rebuild. They were much more successful in rebuilding the School's fortunes than their own, which were to sink from bad to worse over the next eighty years.

The new school building arose just half-way through the School's three centuries in the city. At last we can see what it looked like: several drawings and engravings survive. John Strype, the antiquary, gives us a description of the old School, which he had attended, and says the new one was similar. He was writing many years later, and it is not altogether clear where he is describing the old building and where the new. At any rate, the new building was longer and wider and also lighter at first, with overhead light provided from a louvre, removed at the end of the century. In its early days, the boys played in the ruins of the Cathedral, where rebuilding only began in 1675, and which, when completed, overshadowed the School from thirty feet across the way.

An influential educational historian, William Boyd, argued that the practical effect of humanist reform on schools was short-lived; very soon the classical authors

*The schoolroom in 1697: Colet's bust can be seen over the High Master's chair. A companion drawing of the exterior shows that the louvre, prominently shown here, was in the process of demolition.*

studied, and the new textbooks devised to help study them, were taught with the same rigid tyranny as the medieval curriculum: the liberator had become the gaoler. A 'second renaissance' was needed, and the dawning of such a renaissance Boyd finds in the empirical and practical thinking of Montaigne, Bacon and Locke. He also gives an honourable place to Mulcaster and Milton. Boyd was well aware that, in schools, this second renaissance too was something of a false dawn. It is not easy to see much connexion between what Gill and Mulcaster wrote and the stories about their schoolroom practice. But during the seventeenth century there may really have been a change of sensibility, a shift, as Laurence Stone has argued, from patriarchal severity towards more openly expressed intimacy and affection in family life, which touched school life too. It may, on the other hand, be an illusion, created by the increasing number of surviving records, if not by selective use of them. At St Paul's, the Great Fire is a watershed: after it we have the first surviving library catalogue (1697) the first surviving school timetable (between 1672 and 1697) and what may be the first surviving nominal roll (1697–8).

The documents from the late seventeenth century suggest little or no lessening of the commitment to classical literature and traditional methods. Every day began at 7 a.m. with Latin prayers and a chapter from the Bible. Saturday was for catechizing and forming verbs. The junior forms spent almost all their time at Latin; Greek was begun in the sixth form, and Hebrew in the eighth. Cromleholme, Gale and Postlethwayte were all well known as Hebrew scholars, and Gale and Postlethwayte as Arabic scholars too. Gale had been Regius Professor of Greek at Cambridge when he was appointed in 1672, and in 1697 he was promoted to the Deanery of York.

Yet surely a new air is blowing through the new building. These High Masters are not the famous floggers that their predecessors had been. Indeed, when young John Strype, a delicate boy, ran away to escape a whipping from the Surmaster, and was sent to Merchant Taylors', Cromleholme himself reassured him and brought him back, not to be touched again. Cromleholme also took pains over arranging exhibitions for able poor boys, and his welcome, a few months before his death, to a new boarder from Lancashire, suggests a kind heart. He sent the boy's mother his love. He called up his wife, and said 'Sweetheart, you must take this child as mine and yours'. He was glad to hear he was 'past the measels and smallpox. After we had drunk a glass or two of ale about, he laid his hand on the boy's head and blessed him.' Gale was a Fellow of the Royal Society and friend of Aubrey, Evelyn and Pepys (whose cousin he married and with whom he corresponded on the history of ship-building). Halley was his Captain of the School in 1673; while still at school (as Aubrey was told by Mr Haxton, the globe-maker) 'he was very perfect in the caelestiall Globes ... if a star were misplaced in the Globe, he would presently find it'. Postlethwayte had been Headmaster of the new school of St Martin-in-the-Fields, whose foundation was an important part of the pastoral strategy of its vicar, Thomas Tenison. Its aim was to educate, and clothe and feed, the children of the poor; their apprenticeship would then be paid for. In 1694 Tenison became Archbishop of Canterbury, and it was mainly his influence that secured Postlethwayte's appointment to St Paul's, but Richard Bentley, the great classical scholar, also testified to his learning. In 1699 the Archbishop of Tuam wrote to thank Postlethwayte for his kindness to his sons while at the School, and for corresponding with them after they had left. Another former pupil wrote to Postlethwayte describing his adventures on an embassy to the Barbary Coast. It rather looks as if, for over half a century, the School was ruled by a succession of three kindly, as well as learned, men.

*Thomas Gale, from a portrait at Trinity College, Cambridge. Gale was Fellow of Trinity and Regius Professor of Greek, until his election as High Master in 1672.*

YOU are desired to accompany the Corps of the Reverend Mr. John Postlethwayt, from his late Dwelling-house in S. Paul's Church-yard, to the Parish-Church of S. Austin, on Wednesday next, the 30th of September, 1713. at Four of the Clock in the Afternoon, by reason there will be a Sermon.

Pray bring this Ticket with you.

*Those who accepted this invitation will have heard a sermon entitled 'The Christian Schoolmaster'. According to an obituary written the day after the funeral, the High Master's conscientiousness hastened his death, as almost to the end 'he sent for his Boarders up to his bedside, to read their Chapters, as usual, out of the Greek and Latin Testament'.*

# V

## 'IT IS HOPED IT WILL SOON REGAIN ITS FORMER FLOURISHING STATE'

*Charles Crumpe, Clerk to the Mercers' Company –*
*advertisement in the press 1748*

### 1713–1824

HIGH MASTER POSTLETHWAYTE was a bachelor, his nephew Matthew, an Old Pauline, was Archdeacon of Norwich, and Matthew's daughter married a Norfolk parson, Samuel Kerrich, who was also an Old Pauline. Owing to these unremarkable facts there survive among the parish records of Dersingham, where Kerrich was vicar for nearly forty years, several lists of boys at St Paul's School.

The largest of these lists, which dates from 1697–8, contains 146 names, and it is therefore tempting to believe it to be a complete school list – the earliest complete list we have. If so, the School was bottom-heavy: there are seventy boys in the first form (average age nine), and only four in the seventh (average age fourteen) and three in the eighth (average age seventeen). The youngest boys are seven (three of them) and the oldest seventeen (two). Another list among the same papers, which probably dates from 1693, gives eighth- and seventh-formers only – seven eighth- and nine seventh-formers.

All the names on the main list have a date of admission, and these run fairly evenly over a year (except for August and December, probably holiday months). It may therefore, especially given the very large numbers of juniors, be an admissions list. In that case either the School was hugely swollen or the turnover was very rapid. Postlethwayte had beds in his house for sixteen boarders: but what are they among so many? Were boys being admitted for a brief period (despite the Governors' ruling, repeated that very year) to secure exhibitions at the universities? Did parents value a year or two's schooling for their sons, but see no need for too much of a good thing? Or was somebody making a profit out of admissions despite the recent reiteration of the Statute which ruled that nothing was to be charged beyond the payment, now a shilling, for the porter-boy?

The Dersingham lists pose more problems than they solve, but they do give us some solid information. Age did not determine place in the School: there is a second-former of thirteen and a seventh-former of twelve. Most Paulines were Londoners: the list includes the *patria* of the first twenty-six and then gives up: twenty-four are from London, one is from Essex and one is from Dublin. (However, Postlethwayte's obituarist claims that 'he had scholars sent to him not only from most parts of these Kingdoms, but also from our plantations in the West Indies, and some few even from the Eastern parts of the world'.) Of 164 names altogether in the Dersingham papers, only twenty-four can be identified with previously known Paulines. Lost Paulines must be legion. At the end of the seventeenth century the School was either not quite full or it was overflowing. Either way, it had no lack of little boys.

Half a century later there were only thirty-five boys in the School. The ages of four of these are unknown. Of the rest, the oldest was fourteen and the youngest seven. The average was between nine and ten. Far from admitting only boys who could 'rede and write competently', St Paul's may have been teaching the ABC.

There is a consensus that traditional educational institutions declined in the eighteenth century, though whether the reality was failure within or changing demands is hard to say. Very much the same problem applies to the Church, which was deeply involved in these institutions, and just as historical revisionists are now suggesting that we think again about the standard picture of the eighteenth-century Church, so we must beware of the stereotype in thinking about eighteenth-century schools. Of the four great schools whose arms are shown on the title page of William Walker's *Treatise on English Particles* (1673), St Paul's had the weakest formal ties with the Church, yet most eighteenth-century masters there were in Orders, and so were very large numbers of Old Paulines – twenty-six of the fifty-five identified from High Master Morland's time (1721–33), for instance. It is tempting to relate the sharp decline in the School's fortune to the eclipse of the Tories, the Church party, after the death of Queen Anne: but the two major Pauline statesmen of the early eighteenth century, Marlborough and Spencer Compton, though both from Tory families, ended up the one allied to the Whigs and the other incorporated in them. Compton, *premier manqué* in 1727, was First Lord of the Treasury during the last few months of his life (1742–3). In 1724, Samuel Knight, emboldened by Compton's 'known affection' for the School, dedicated his *Life of Colet* to him, rather tactlessly explaining that though 'we have lately lost two persons of the most exalted stations that our School could glory in, viz. the Dukes of Marlborough and Manchester . . . we have still a patron in you'.

But the School not only lost its aristocratic patrons by death, it ceased to attract any more. This happened quite suddenly, and the significant date is not the death of Queen Anne in 1714, but the death of Postlethwayte the year before. No more

*A teaching aid known as a hornbook, though this one is metal: depressing evidence, if really used at St Paul's, of the School's standards for admission in the 1720s.*

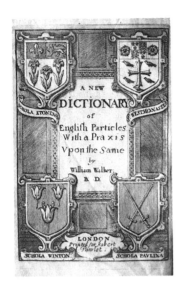

*The eleventh edition of Walker's English Particles, 1695, shows the arms of the four great schools of the day, with St Paul's in fourth place. The arms assigned to St Paul's are, unusually, those of the See of London. The School has no arms of its own, but uses those of the Founder, and is from time to time upbraided by purists for doing so.*

Opposite: *Benjamin Morland, High Master, by John Smibert, painted not later than 1728, when Smibert left England for America.*

noblemen's sons are to be found until General Campbell, a cousin of the Duke of Argyll who chanced to succeed to the dukedom, put his two sons under his fellow Scotchman, High Master Charles, in the 1730s. Nor, when the School revived after Charles's dismal reign, did it ever regain the favour of the *haut monde*. Church dignitaries too appear to have stopped sending their sons to St Paul's in this period.

Philip Ayscough was a sick man when chosen as High Master in 1713, and resigned 'in decay of spirits, vigour and strength', as he put it, eight years later. Very much an 'in-house' appointment, he was an Old Pauline, and had been Surmaster since 1685. He was also probably a Whiggish appointment; the three bishops who recommended him, though of diverse politics, were all committed to the Hanoverian succession; on leaving St Paul's, he received a comfortable living from King George I, and a good pension from the Mercers, and lived another twenty years. In October 1713 a Whig appointment was against the swing: there was a Tory landslide in the General Election taking place that very month. But the Mercers, who nominated strong Whigs as Apposers in 1713 and 1714, were clearly already Whiggish, even before the long years of Whiggery about to begin. Arthur Ashley Sykes, a latudinarian polemicist 'whose whole life was a warfare of the pen', preached a sermon at Cambridge in 1716 which scandalized his High Church fellow Pauline, Edward Rud: 'perhaps the like was never heard before in any place'. Sykes was an Apposer almost every year from 1733 to 1756.

In 1721 a candidate for the High Mastership thought it worth advertising in the press that the rumour that he was a Jacobite was a parcel of vile untruths. He was unsuccessful. In 1734, a year of vehement anti-clerical agitation in parliament, the Governors ordered that prayers should no longer be read in Latin, but in English, and by the Chaplain, not the Captain of the School (or High Lad, as he was sometimes called in this period). This order, if obeyed at all, may not have lasted long. Ten years later, the Chaplain, who was already often called Usher or Under-usher, was submerged altogether in these secular titles. In 1763 prayers were to be read, four times a day, 'by one of the Scholars of the Upper Class'. Only one of the masters was obliged to be present.

All this fashionable Low-Church Whiggery does not seem to have done the School any good. It may have been mainly an expression of the Mercers' determination to keep the usually clerical schoolmasters under control. Ayscough, who had already unsuccessfully applied for the High Mastership in 1697, and whose teaching had come in for some criticism – he was said to have little Greek and Latin and no Hebrew – may have seemed malleable. The Governors at once deprived him of the right to appoint the Surmaster, and in 1721 even transferred the power to promote boys from form to form from the High Master to the Surveyor Accountant. They used their power to continue, and intensify, a policy of internal promotion. Between 1703 and 1733 five Chaplains were appointed; all were Old Paulines (as were nine out of thirteen in the whole century). Eight eighteenth-century Chaplains or Ushers were promoted to the Surmastership, one of these subsequently to the High Mastership; one (Timothy Crumpe) rose to be High Master direct. Between 1673 and 1864 nine Surmasters, eight of them Old Paulines, were from Trinity College, Cambridge. Only three (out of seven)

Though James Greenwood was, in 1737, twice rebuked by the Court of Assistants, for lateness and for drinking, his grammatical works were very successful, and no doubt lucrative. The London Vocabulary, which was attractively illustrated, went into twenty-two editions by the end of the century. The School Library possesses sixteen copies, several of them autographed and doodled on by Paulines.

John Ayres. 'That excellent penman', wrote Addison, 'had taken care to affix his portrait to the title-page of his learned treatise' (The Tutor to Penmanship, 1698).

eighteenth-century High Masters were Old Paulines: but there have only been four altogether. Understandable when things were going well, this looks a strange appointments policy when the School was going downhill.

A different policy was tried from time to time. Benjamin Morland, High Master from 1721 to 1733, had no previous connection with the School. Before he came to St Paul's, he had made a great success of a private boarding school in Hackney; this continued to flourish under his successor and son-in-law, the Pauline Henry Newcombe, but not for much longer. Morland may have been appointed to St Paul's to arrest the decline begun under Ayscough, and he may have had some success in doing so. He was almost certainly a layman, and the Surmaster who joined him the next year, James Greenwood, was not only a layman but apparently a non-graduate. Greenwood had some enlightened ideas: he believed in the education of girls, and he attacked the practice of teaching children grammar in Latin, 'before they have learned any thing of it in English'. He himself wrote a very successful English Grammar, as well as an anthology of English verse, *The Virgin Muse*, dedicated to several young ladies of his acquaintance. Though his works are not included in a published list of *Books used in the Lower Forms of St Paul's School* (1722), it is clear that some teaching, at least, was done in English in this period: and necessarily, for in 1730 the Chaplain, stung by a rebuke from the Apposers, declared that he had ninety boys in his care, that most of them were very young, and that many of them 'had not read in the Accidence before they came to him' – they needed precisely what Greenwood was trying to provide.

The School was also providing, on the side, instruction in penmanship and accountancy. In 1583 Harrison had asked for the appointment of a writing-master, but without success; similarly, a proposal to let a room to a writing-master in 1675 had come to nothing; but from about that date until the early nineteenth century a series of distinguished penmen were associated with the School, if not exactly employed by it. The first, John Ayres (known as the Colonel), published the *Paul's School Round Hand* in 1700. His pupil, John Rayner, followed this up with *The Paul's Scholars' Copy Book* in 1709. Although the town was 'already glutted with Copy-Books,' he wrote, 'the Reverend and learned Master [Postlethwayte] did frequently invite me to publish some Alphabets etc. of the Learned Languages taught there'. In the 1720s some of the collection at the Feast Sermon was allocated to teaching limited numbers of boys writing and arithmetic; but the writing-masters advertised, and were probably entrepreneurs rather than employees. One of them, John Clark, had been at Merchant Taylors', where Greenwood may also have been at school: they arrived at St Paul's at about the same time. Greenwood's English Grammar was 'printed for John Clark at the Bible and Crown in the Poultry, near Cheapside'; so perhaps the writing-master diversified. His son went to school at St Paul's, then to Cambridge, and holy orders and the Chaplaincy, and succeeded Greenwood as Surmaster in 1737. Thus he exemplified the traditional grammar school cursus, summarized in an *Ode to St Paul* by one formerly of St Paul's School (1702):

> . . . and when from hence we bear thy Name
> To sing thy Praise, on Isis Banks or Cam:

44

From thee will learn as Genius shall incline
To be PHYSITIAN, LAWYER, or DIVINE.

However, beautiful as were the scripts they taught, the writing-masters are probably a sign that the parents of many Paulines were mainly interested in getting
their sons a useful, practical training for the life of a city shopkeeper or skilled
tradesman. By 1862, when there had long ceased to be a writing-master, the High
Master wished there was one, and described the boys' handwriting as dreadful.
He blamed the new metal pens.

Morland's successor, Timothy Crumpe, was conventional in all respects (St
Paul's, Trinity, ordination, Chaplain), except that he jumped straight from the
Chaplaincy, and that, at thirty-three, he was the youngest applicant. The Mercers
had already shown their approval of him when, in 1729, they made him Chaplain
to the Company. He was conscientious and, apparently, successful. But he died
less than four years later, in 1737, and the Governors then made a surprising, even
mysterious, and almost fatal choice.

George Charles is the only High Master (apart from Freeman, whose place of
education is unknown) who was neither an Oxford nor a Cambridge man. He
was a graduate of Marischal College, Aberdeen. If, as is likely, he was a member
of the Church of Scotland, his appointment must have seemed an affront to the
Dean and Chapter, and to the High Church Bishop of London, Edmund Gibson:
it may not be a coincidence that Gibson had broken with the all-powerful minister,
Robert Walpole, the year before – offending him did not matter as much as it
had done. The Scots were unpopular in eighteenth-century England, generally
regarded as needy adventurers on the make: in 1697 the first point noted against
an unsuccessful candidate for the High Mastership was 'Scotchman bred if not
born'; it was feared that he would 'make his sons Ushers, with design to rivett

*John Clark, writing-master at St
Paul's about 1720, from the second
edition of his* Writing Improved,
or Penmanship made easy in its
useful and ornamental parts, with
various examples in all the hands.

## ALPHABETUM HEBRAICUM.

| Potestas | Nomen | Figura | | | Potestas | Nomen | Figura | |
|---|---|---|---|---|---|---|---|---|
| L | Lamed | לָמֶד | ל | | A *Aspiratio le- nissima* | Aleph | אָלֶף | א |
| M | Mem | מֵם | מ | | β *sive N euphonans* | Beth | בֵּית | ב |
| N | Nun | נוּן | נ | | Gh | Gimel | גִּימֶל | ג |
| S | Samech | סָמֶךְ | ס | | Dh | Daleth | דָּלֶת | ד |
| *Aspiratio dens issima* Aijn | | עַיִן | ע | | H | He | הֵא | ה |
| Ph | Pe | פֵּא | פ | | V *euphonans* | Vau | וָו | ו |
| Tf | Tfade | צָדִי | צ | | Z *vel S* | Zaijn | זַיִן | ז |
| Q *vel K* | Coph | קוֹף | ק | | Hh *vel* χ | Cheth | חֵית | ח |
| R | Refc | רֵישׁ | ר | | T | Teth | טֵית | ט |
| S *vel Sc* | Scin | שִׁין | שׁ | | J *euphonans* | Jod | יוֹד | י |
| Th *vel* | Tau | תָּו | ת | | Ch | Caph | כַּף | כ |

LITERÆ FINALES.
ץ ף ן ם ך
*Tsade Phe Nun Mem Caph*

LITERÆ EXTENTÆ.
א ב ה ל מ ת
*Aleph Beth He Lamed Mem Tau*

*The Hebrew alphabet, from
Rayner's* Paul's Scholars' Copy
Book. *It is dedicated to the Master
and Wardens of the Mercers and to
High Master Postlethwayte, and
'chiefly Designed for the Use of the
above mencōn'd SCHOOL (that
Celebrated Seat of Learning)'.*

his Family in succession', and that the boarders would see too much of his grown-up daughters. None the less, Charles, who had, so far as is known, no teaching experience, had nearly won the contest for the High Mastership in 1733, and was now easily victorious over four other candidates. Charles was perhaps already friendly with his later patron, Lord Hardwicke; Hardwicke, who had attended a school at Bethnal Green kept by High Master Morland's brother, became Lord Chancellor in February 1737, precisely when Charles became High Master.

That his appointment was utterly disastrous may not have been apparent for some years. It is not known when the slide in numbers began, though it seems possible that in 1729 the School was still more or less full. But by 1744 numbers were down to eighty, and the rest of Charles's time was a landslide: in 1745 there were seventy-two pupils, in 1746, sixty-five, in 1747, sixty-three, in February 1748, fifty-four, and in May, thirty-five. The first recorded complaint of the Governors was comparatively venial: Charles must not presume to fix the dates of the beginning and end of term himself. However, in 1742, John Clark, the Surmaster, claimed that the High Master had threatened to pull him by the nose and (but for his cloth) to kick him about the School; and two years later Joshua Tillotson, the Chaplain, claimed that Charles had treated him with so much public contempt that a senior boy had dared to strike him. The boy's father retorted that the Chaplain was 'Proud, Worthless and insignificant, Passionate, Turbulent and cross'. He thought that 'no Gentleman, who can afford to pay for his son's education, will send him to St Paul's School, to be buffeted about by the Under Masters'. The Governors did their best to reconcile Charles and his staff, ordering solemnly that 'the Scholars should not assault any of the Masters'.

It is extraordinary that, while this civil war was raging, the Apposers, year after year, reported that all was well, and still more extraordinary that these same Apposers, Dr Sykes and Mr Arrowsmith, should have gone on being invited after Charles's departure. In 1746 the boys were 'in very good order'; in 1747 'there was due care taken by all the masters', and 'the children in general were in a very good way'. All the same, the Governors did rather plaintively express the hope that the Masters would 'do their duty with unanimity as a means to restore the school to its former flourishing state'. That they did nothing more for so long would be incredible – except that the Mercers' Company was, in these very years, wobbling on the brink of financial ruin, and thus could neither afford additional scandal nor spare very much thought, perhaps, for the fortunes of the School.

None the less, when the father of a boy called William Roberts brought a formal complaint, with a surgeon's affidavit, 'that Charles had inflicted on his son a "most severe correction of a great number of Stripes on his Back and Face, inflicted with the utmost violence"', it was impossible not to take action. After hearing evidence from several boys, largely turning on the question of whether Roberts had called the High Master 'a white liver coloured Son of a Bitch', the Court of Assistants decided that Charles must go. This was in May 1747. They finally got rid of him in July 1748. It is hardly surprising that only one candidate applied to succeed him. It is surprising, on the other hand, even with the favour of Lord Hardwicke, that Charles went on first to a series of posts in the diplomatic service, and then in 1759 to be tutor to the Prince of Wales's younger brothers, the Dukes of Glouces-

*In John Rocque's map of London (published in 1747) the School, though far from prominent, is clearly identified to the right of the Cathedral.*

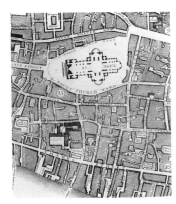

ter and Cumberland. Odder still is that the Prince's own tutor, Francis Ayscough, was probably a close relation of Philip Ayscough, the former High Master.

The first half of the eighteenth century was a period of great financial difficulty for the City of London in general and the Mercers' Company in particular. The Fire had not only destroyed uninsured property: it had made it necessary to give leases on very easy terms. The Mercers, already seriously weakened by the financial demands of James I and Charles I, fell deeper into debt. They made matters worse by an unfortunate scheme for offering annuities to the widows of needy clergymen. Intended to solve all their financial problems, this brought them to the edge of bankruptcy by 1746. As their problems worsened, they borrowed more and more from the Colet estate. In 1714 they owed it £13,531. By 1745 this had risen to £34,637. Statutory obligations to the School continued to be met, and sometimes more than met, but staff salaries remained the same from 1700 to 1749, and the Chapel was not rebuilt after the Fire. In 1675 there were plans for a new school library, as the existing one was 'inconvenient and rendered much worse by the continual noise of Coaches and Carts passing by and by the Dust which spoyles the books and choakes the persons who stay in it'. These were not carried out. The books were still dusty in 1803, and 'defaced by the boys with ink and erasures'. Worst of all, exhibitions at the universities funded by the Colet estate ceased altogether between 1720 and 1748. Those given by individual benefactors continued, and there were some new ones, the Perry exhibitions at Trinity College, Cambridge. But even the Campden exhibitions ceased from 1744 to 1755.

The rapid recovery of the School after the dismissal of Charles is usually attributed to Charles's failings and the merits of his successor, George Thicknesse, and there is certainly truth in that. But it cannot be a coincidence that it was in 1748 that the Mercers obtained an Act of Parliament that helped them out of their financial abyss, to smooth the way for which the Company made a 'speedy investment . . . expressly on trust for St Paul's School' and reconsidered its management of the Colet accounts. Their fortunes also improved naturally in the second half of the century as many leases fell in and property values rose. They seem to have forgotten about their debt to the School until 1804; but they were at least, in the second half of the eighteenth century, in a position to manage its affairs without being distracted by the imminent collapse of their own.

On his appointment, the new High Master was asked to make a list of all the boys on the Foundation, and to record the admission of all subsequently admitted to it. This list has been kept continuously since 1748, so that that year begins a new era in the School's history in two senses. It is not a perfect list: it omits the names of some, perhaps many, non-Foundationers (fee-paying boys admitted by private arrangement with the High Master). Many of these later secured places on the Foundation; but those who did not seldom stayed at St Paul's long, and their parentage, and age and address, are not given. These details are usually, but not always, provided for Foundationers. Despite these reservations, with the beginning of these registers the mid-eighteenth-century Pauline emerges into a good deal of light.

He was, more often than not, the small son of a city tradesman. His average age, on admission, was ten, and he was likely to leave before he was fourteen,

*The bust of George Thicknesse,*
*High Master 1748–69.*

though many stayed longer and a few joined the School at fourteen or fifteen. In June 1753 Charles Stayner entered the School; at five years old he was perhaps the youngest Pauline ever. As the son of a watchmaker, of Ave Mary Lane, off Ludgate Street, he was less unusual; the fifty-nine Foundationers who entered in 1758 included the sons of a bookbinder, an innkeeper, a picture frame-maker, a hair-seller, a pamphlet-seller, a herald-painter, a Doctor of Divinity, two excise-men, a tallow-chandler, a japanner and a mathematical instrument-maker. John Bullevant's father was dead, and his mother kept a school, a more conventional occupation for an eighteenth-century woman than that followed by the mother of Isaac Hooper, who came to St Paul's in September 1756: she was a plumber.

Nearly all the 1758 entrants lived in or near the city. One came from Piccadilly and one from Strand-on-the-Green. Two were the sons of country parsons (from Essex and Suffolk). One, who seems to have died before being admitted, was from Nottinghamshire. In 1768 John Edwards, 'an orphan from Bengal', joined the School, and the father of James Boyle (1762) was in Jamaica. The High Masters and some of their staff took in boarders, and some boys probably stayed as lodgers in neighbouring houses, such as those of the writing-masters.

The speed with which Thicknesse refilled the School is remarkable. It was full again in a year, and soon above the statutory numbers. The imbalance in the forms remained, however: even in 1806 the four senior forms altogether had about the same number of boys as the fourth form, and in 1815 the Apposers thought there were far too many junior boys. Thicknesse's pupils were probably also of a humbler social background than at any other time in the School's history. There were a few sons of clergymen and attorneys, and a very few 'gentlemen' and 'esquires'. These grew more numerous by the end of the century, but for the rest of its life in the City (and beyond) Paulines came from a very extensive social spectrum, and St Paul's was the agent of plenty of upward mobility. As late as 1816 it was included in the purview of a Commons Committee on the Education of the Lower Orders in the Metropolis. Henry Soames (1799), Anglo-Saxonist, Bampton Lec-turer and Chancellor of St Paul's Cathedral, was the son of a shoe-maker. Jonathan Pollock (1800) Attorney General and Lord Chief Baron of the Exchequer, was the son of a saddler. William Jobbins (1780), on the other hand, who was the son of a customs officer, was hanged for arson and robbery ten years after he entered St Paul's.

Entry to the Foundation was now firmly in the hands of the Surveyor Accountant, who was usually the outgoing Master of the Mercers' Company. As he changed every year there is unlikely to have been any long-term admissions policy. To provide for the additional numbers which resulted from the admission of non-Foundationers, or perhaps just to cope with the crowd of small boys in the junior forms, an additional master was regularly appointed by the High Master from 1750, and paid by him. The Governors began to subsidize the wages of this master in 1773 and finally took over his appointment and pay in 1814; from then until 1876 they allowed no more non-Foundationers to be admitted. Numbers, which had again fallen below a hundred around the turn of the century, thus remained at or around the statutory 153 almost until the School left the City of London.

Unlike his predecessor, High Master Thicknesse seems to have got on well with his employers, his colleagues and his pupils. That the reports of the Apposers were generally glowing may not mean much, since they were, at first, the same Apposers who had glowed about Charles; Sykes was an Apposer in the year of his death, 1756, after which his brother founded an exhibition in his memory. Only occasionally are the Apposers' reports recorded in anything but the briefest generalities: the School is 'in a very flourishing way', in 'as good order as ever they saw it': but in 1757 they find that the junior classes were 'very well grounded in the Grammar Rules', and that the seniors 'went very well through their Examination in the several Authors they had learned; and they found the School, in general, better than they expected'.

More significant were the improved relations between the Governors and the High Master. True, he was occasionally reprimanded. In 1755 he was ordered to break up for the holidays (which began then at Christmas, Easter, Whitsun and Bartholomewtide – late August) on Saturday mornings and not on Fridays. In 1760 he admitted to having accepted a present of two dozen bottles of wine, and was told not to do so again. But it is apparent that the Mercers had confidence in Thicknesse. When he fell ill in 1758, and had to spend a few months in Bath, they gave him fifty guineas for his expenses there, and another fifty the following year, with warm praise for his hard work, which they clearly thought was a cause of his indisposition. It may indeed have been a mental breakdown: as an old pupil recalled it, much later: 'the victories of that memorable year were ringing through the themes and verses of the seventh and eighth class boys', when, while hearing the seniors' translations, Thicknesse himself began to babble about siege-warfare, and had to be taken away by his brother. The setting in the year of Victories (1759) is wrong; one must not put too much faith in Old Boys' reminiscences. Whatever really happened, the Governors' trust in Thicknesse was not diminished. In 1769, when he insisted on retiring because, he said, his memory was failing him, they accepted his resignation reluctantly. According to McDonnell he was asked to name his successor, but in fact an election was held as usual.

Though the Mercers' own financial problems were far from over, with the Act of 1748 they had turned the corner, and were able to take a more active and enterprising interest in the School. They inaugurated an enquiry into the Colet Trust

*Above: Silver medal designed by Pingo. Below: Gold medal designed by G. F. Pidgeon, 1800. Most of the medals were awarded to members of the Court of Assistants.*

and its estates; they ordered (surely not before time) that its accounts should be kept in separate books from the rest of their business. They raised the masters' pay and began to award Pauline exhibitions again, periodically reviewing and increasing their value. Recipients had to produce certificates of residence: in 1756 William Chilcott, of Christ's, is allowed leave of absence, on doctor's advice, because he suffers from convulsive fits and needs a change of air, but when in 1771 nine Cambridge exhibitioners petitioned the Court of Assistants, in the most abjectly respectful language, that the rules of residence should be relaxed to allow them the same vacations as the rest of the university, their request was unanimously rejected and they were 'severely reprimanded from the chair for sending so insolent a memorial to the Court'. Five years later, in response to a request from High Master Roberts, the Court did agree to change the rules. The Governors also ordered books for the library (Chaucer, Bacon and Locke, as well as classical authors), agreed to take a lease of two houses in Old Change to enlarge the school premises, as 'the Buildings behind St Paul's School are so close, and the Yard . . . so narrow and confined as to render the school very incommodious and even unwholesome', and got Thicknesse to agree to the partition of the High Master's house at Stepney – he should keep the half he chose, and the other half should be let to the benefit of the Colet estate. In 1754 they decided to give prizes (with a maximum value of £5) 'for the encouragement of the Scholars'. They then got rather carried away with enthusiasm, and enlarged the scheme into an annual award of six medals, three gold and three silver (total cost £38 9s. 8d.), but eventually caution prevailed: only two gold medals were awarded, and Mr Pingo, of Hatton Garden, the engraver, was closely examined about the amount of gold he needed. From 1787 a silver medal was presented annually to the Surveyor Accountant instead. It was not until 1813 that book prizes, one for the best boy in each class, began to be awarded at Apposition.

Philip Francis, the recipient of one of the gold medals, was a boarder, and Captain of the School in 1755. An archetypal swot, he had earlier been warned by his father not to press the High Master for promotion:

> I rejoice with you at being so long head of your class, and I hope you will enjoy your superiority over your class-fellows by condescension, compliance, and, if they desire it, by assisting them. . . . When you come into the world you must hide whatever superiority you possess.

This advice Francis in later years conspicuously failed to follow, but he remembered Thicknesse as 'the wisest, learnedest, quietest and best man he ever knew', helped support him in his old age, and got Burke to advise on the Latin of his epitaph. Thicknesse used to say 'that some boys had no talent for the acquisition of the dead languages, and that a master must be content with their elementary instruction'. John Bowyer Nichols, the antiquary and literary gossip, who entered St Paul's, aged eleven, a week or two before Thicknesse's death, said that 'he considered boys as rational beings' and 'raised the school to the highest reputation without the use of the rod'.

He does not say whether the other masters, who taught hordes of small boys, as opposed to the High Master's ten or twenty seniors, also abandoned corporal punishment; but Thicknesse had alleviated their task by the appointment of the Assistant, who helped with the first and second forms. The first Assistant soon departed for Saint Saviour's Grammar School, Southwark; but the second, Richard Roberts, served Thicknesse for seventeen years and succeeded him as High Master. He had first entered St Paul's as a small boy, probably about 1738. He resigned the High Mastership in 1814. Thus not only was this the longest High Mastership by far, but, boy, Assistant and High Master, he was at St Paul's for seventy-two of the ninety-four years of his life. It looks, too, as if he was not eager to retire, even at eighty-five: his departure was eased by a pension of £1000 a year, £400 more than his effective salary. Towards the end, he certainly let things slide. There was a half-hearted attempt to get rid of him in 1809. Immediately after he did resign, the Apposers made pointed suggestions for improving the syllabus, especially in religious instruction.

Roberts was the last Old Pauline High Master. Both the Surmasters appointed in his day, two out of the four Under-ushers and five of the six Assistants whose names are known, were Paulines too. In fact, every Surmaster except one from 1783 to 1864 was a Pauline, as was every Under-usher (from 1824 called, more politely, Third Master) from 1763 to 1861. There were not many of these men; they stayed a long time. In the twenty-one years' High Mastership of Roberts' successor, John Sleath, throughout which there were always four masters altogether, only five men taught at St Paul's: Sleath, Edwards, Durham, Cooper, Bean. Edwards was Surmaster for forty years (1783–1823); Durham (an Old Pauline) taught as Under-usher and then Surmaster for thirty-one years (1806–37). Cooper (an Old Pauline) was Fourth and Third Master from 1824 to 1861 (thirty-seven years); Bean, Assistant to the High Master and then Surmaster, put in thirty-nine years, from 1813 to 1852.

They were all clergymen, and they and their School look, from this distance, like small pillars of that vigorous and confident (or, if you reject the revisionist view, stagnant and complacent) church-state which was the England of George III and his sons. George III would have approved of Roberts's correction of a boy's poem written to celebrate Trafalgar:

> 'Presumptuous thought!' Britannia's genius cries;
> 'Rise, my loved sons, my brave defenders, rise;
> Tell them, while each with emulation strives –
> Though Nelson falls, a Collingwood survives.'

This last line, the High Master felt, showed insufficient respect for rank. He corrected it to:

> 'Though Nelson falls, Lord Collingwood survives'.

That, at any rate, is the story the author told. He was R. H. Barham, Captain of the School in 1806, and later Senior Cardinal of St Paul's Cathedral and enormously popular as a comic poet and connoisseur of absurdity. A few years later another Pauline, William Henry Medhurst, had a more direct and brutal encounter with the war at sea. He left school to join the Navy, suffered an amputation, and was reinstated at the School in 1811. Roberts, despite his sense of hierarchy, received honours from neither Church nor State; but Sleath was made prebendary of St Paul's (1822), Chaplain in Ordinary to the King (1825) and Sub-dean of the Chapel Royal (1833). Sleath's duties at Court sometimes required him to leave school early on Wednesday afternoons. 'These occasions', a pupil of his recalled, 'were looked forward to with a good deal of satisfaction. Some of the more audacious of the Eighth used to slope away home at once.'

It is cynically said of papal elections that a principal qualification of the new pope is that he should be as unlike the previous pope as possible. It could be argued that this was also true at the end of each of the long High Masterships during the last years of the English *ancien régime*. Thicknesse was successful and respected, and did without flogging. Roberts appears to have mixed kindly ineffectiveness with ferocious onslaughts: 'a venerable-looking man, at least in his last days, seeming scarce more lively than in his bust, which now adorns the school-room, except when plying the cane; and on such occasions he was wonderfully active, as if inspired by new life'. Yet the same writer recalls that he could not stop the boys 'throwing books at the head of everyone, whoever he was, who entered the school-room with his hat on his head'.

Sleath hardly ever used the cane – he did not need to: 'his very shadow seemed to send a shudder through your frame from head to foot'. The writer (later a distinguished Jesuit) remembers Sleath punishing only once, 'and that very terribly. It was a case of a boy having appropriated what did not belong to him.' The beating – like everything else that happened in lesson times it took place in front

*Frontispiece to* The Ingoldsby Legends *by 'Thomas Ingoldsby' (R. H. Barham) published by his schoolfellow, Richard Bentley. Cruikshank shows Barham surrounded by the monstrous creation of his imagination, while Bentley peers anxiously over his left elbow.*

of the whole school – 'was something never to be forgotten. A boy by my side in the Seventh, more sensitive than most, sank down on the form, and covered his face with his hands.' Sleath, 'tall and corpulent, and very upright, as all corpulent men must be, to keep the centre of gravity far enough back for stability of equilibrium', was succeeded in 1838 by Kynaston, of whom McDonnell wrote: 'He abolished the birch-rod, but appears to have been unable to replace it by moral suasion.'

That takes us from the late Georgian to the early Victorian, the Dickensian, age. For while Kynaston was a poet of Tractarian and antiquarian sensibilities, Sleath and his staff are, or could be made to appear, Dickensian figures. A few months before Dickens immortalized Whackford Squeers, W. A. Campbell Durham, known, by no means merely acronymously, as Whack Durham, or the immortal Whack, resigned the Surmastership.

> He always had his cane in hand, except when he threw it at a boy's head; and he was constantly finding reasons for using it . . . from time to time word would be passed round. 'Durham's in a wax; mind and laugh at his puns' . . . He taught us nothing. His plan was, not to tell us what was right, but to thrash us till we found it out for ourselves. When we did find it out, we remembered it; this is a point in favour of his plan.

The young Dickens had a number of Pauline connections. He and Barham, who shared his taste for the grotesque, belonged to a literary circle which included John Bowyer Nichols, proprietor of the *Gentleman's Magazine*, and his cousin Richard Bentley; both of them had been at school with Barham, and Barham, as well as Dickens, published his early work in Bentley's magazine, *Bentley's Miscellany*.

William Ballantine, Serjeant at Law, recalls the three masters, Edwards, Durham and Bean as 'all tyrants – cruel, cold-blooded, unsympathetic tyrants'. He presents them as monsters: Durham with 'a face as if cut out of a suet pudding', Edwards 'a cadaverous looking object', who liked caning the boys on their shivering, glove-less fingers, Bean throwing the dictionary at boys who yawned, to cheer himself up. Father Kingdon, the Jesuit, indignantly defends Bean: he was certainly a martinet with precise requirements about ink bottles, but his 'Greek tree' (an exhaustive diagram of every permutation of a Greek verb, to be shown up in red and black on a full sheet of foolscap) gave some of his pupils more pleasure than pain. When Bean – 'dear old man', another Pauline called him – visited Cambridge, all his former pupils there gave him a grand breakfast – which is enough, Kingdon indignantly concludes, to refute Ballantine's unjust judgement.

Affectionate reminiscences of painful schooldays are curiously common: Kingdon himself is aware of the paradox that, while most of what he recalls (in *The Pauline* half a century later) is fairly grim, his overall impression of those days is happy. For Ballantine his first day at St Paul's was 'the blackest and most odious day of my existence'. It was 23 October 1819; he was seven years old. He left when he was about thirteen. On 1 July 1864, he attended the first annual Old Pauline dinner. It was eight years after that, when he was seventy, that he published in his *Reminiscences* his scathing onslaught on the St Paul's of his youth.

# VI

## 'AT ST PAUL'S . . . WE TEACH NOTHING BUT . . .
## LATIN AND GREEK'

*John Sleath*

### 1824–1876

BALLANTINE'S FIRST DAY at the School was not in St Paul's churchyard, but in a warehouse in Aldersgate, where classes were held while the School was being rebuilt. As early as 1763 the High Master had reported the School as 'much out of repair'. On that occasion, prompt action was taken; but as the building aged and the traffic of London increased, the situation could only get worse. In 1782 the Governors turned down a proposal for partial rebuilding. It included 'inclosing the Boys Privies by a cover'd way they now being but an Unpleasing Sight from the Ushers House'. In 1815 the Surmaster complained that his house lacked a WC, and the following year the school privies were reported to be 'very offensive'. (Ninety years and two buildings later, Victor Gollancz thought they still were.) There was a frightening outbreak of scarlet fever in 1820. In 1819 Sleath testified, to Parliamentary Commissioners investigating the administration of charitable trusts: 'The roof of the school is propped up. It was examined a few years since and reported to be unsafe. It is now supported by wooden pillars.' These props and pillars had been put up in 1814, in case the people watching the victory procession from the roof of the School should fall through it. By that date the Governors had been intermittently discussing rebuilding for a decade. It was finally completed in 1824.

That year also saw the final liquidation of the Mercers' Company's debt to the Colet Trust. After its half-century of oblivion the debt had been discovered, the Charity Commissioners quaintly recounted, in an old cash-book of the Surveyor Accountant. In fact the Company, in a thorough financial spring-cleaning begun in 1803 after the last shadows of bankruptcy had been cleared away, had roused this dormant albatross and decided to shoulder it, though not without vehement protests from some of their members. It was unwise, some argued, to admit obligations that might whet the appetites of other claimants. It was unwiser, the majority probably felt, to face a parliament and public beginning to be critical of privileged institutions, without honouring such large and long-standing obligations. In any case, the debt was settled, and the school was rebuilt at a cost of £23,000.

This may have been a mistake. The alternative, which had been canvassed, tentatively approved and at once abandoned by the Court of Assistants in 1810, was to move. It was impossible to provide adequate boarding facilities or playing fields, to expand in any substantial way, without doing so. On the other side was the intimate and historic connexion with the City, and the complexity of the legal position. It appeared that the approval of the Court of Chancery was needed both for a move out of London and for the formal provision of boarding places. The Mercers may also have feared that distance would reduce their control. In 1817

*By the time this engraving (by Howlet of a drawing by John Baker) was published in 1825, the building it depicts had been pulled down. The fourth floors were added to the masters' houses in 1754. Is the gowned figure approaching the Surmaster's door the terrible 'Whack'? Are the boys playing marbles and trundling the hoop Paulines?*

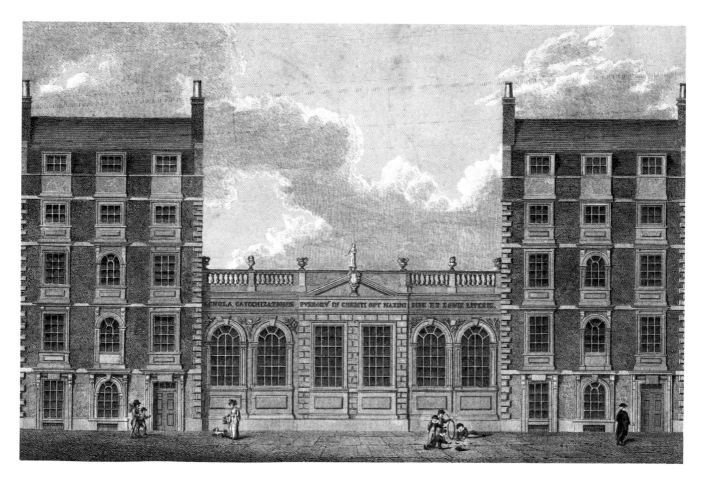

*The schoolroom in 1862. The spiral staircase leads to the Library, where, that very year, the Public Schools Commissioners interviewed the School authorities.*

*The third School building with the Cathedral on the right. Traffic does not appear to be a serious problem, though contemporaries complained of it bitterly.*

and again in 1820 they strongly reasserted it over Sleath, when he objected to the annual indignity of resigning and being reappointed – it was, they assured him, no formality; he was threatened with dismissal and brought to heel. He must have learned his lesson: in 1828 they asked him and his staff to dinner, and presented them with three hundred guineas' worth of plate. Had St Paul's moved out in 1820 it would have been, by half a century, the first of the great London schools to do so, and it might have found, in one jump, the satisfactory site and buildings which two later jumps have not entirely achieved. It might, on the other hand, have lost its soul.

For all its cupola and Greek revival columns, the new School, though larger and grander, was not an immense change from the old. In an intensely, perhaps neurotically, conservative age, and under the direction of intensely, perhaps neurotically, conservative Governors, it hardly could be. James Malcolm, seeking information about the School for a history of London, was frigidly rebuffed by the Mercers in 1803, at which date they may have felt they had something to hide. But Miss M. Hackett's attack on the School in 1816, because she believed that its revenues had been unlawfully diverted from the Cathedral choristers, was strident and unjustified. Her grievance was that of a Church-Tory. There were few real radical breezes to ruffle Bean, that 'rigid *laudator temporis acti*', and his colleagues in their black silk stockings, knee-breeches, top hats and gowns (compulsory from 1775) as they came into the single great schoolroom with their silver candlesticks, not always precisely at seven o'clock in the morning.

The new building was nearly half as long again as the old, taking in properties on its southern end which the Mercers had gradually acquired in the second half of the eighteenth century. Most of the new space was used for housing for the masters: the new schoolroom, though rather broader, was about the same length as the old. It was, however, raised well above street level, to provide a semi-subterranean playground underneath; this had been a feature of the abortive 1782 proposals. From the pavement you could see the boys at play through a grille. Inside the schoolroom the boys sat in tiers on either side of the room, first, third, fifth and seventh classes on one side, second, fourth, sixth and eighth on the other. Their seats also served as lockers: all but the front row now had desks, which Sleath had asked for before the rebuilding. There were four chairs for the four masters, spaced out along the middle of the room. Each master was in charge of two classes: while he taught one, which sat on a horse-shoe arrangement round his chair, his other class would be left to their own devices. They were allowed to work in groups, and if they had finished, or chose to risk not doing, their set tasks, nobody objected to them chatting and playing, if they were not too noisy. This was relative; Kingdon recalls the whole schoolroom being in 'a constant roar, or a loud buzz, which never seemed to incommode anybody; but this made it necessary to speak pretty loud in class, and not very low when studying together'.

'At St Paul's School', said the Doctor in his solemn way, 'we teach nothing but the Classics, nothing but Latin and Greek. If you want your boy to learn anything else you must have him taught at home, and for this purpose we give him three half-holidays per week.' That Sleath's famous words were said with ironical bitterness has generally been missed. Roberts's Hebrew was said to be scanty, and Sleath had abandoned it altogether: but if there was no mathematics taught, this was despite the fact that, immediately he became High Master, Sleath had urged the Governors to appoint a master to teach writing and arithmetic. There must have been some mathematics taught in Barham's time (1800–8), for him to have made no progress in it. But even in the 1840s it was taught to no form lower than the fifth (and indeed on one of the half-holidays, though compulsorily), partly by the Fourth Master, and partly by a derided and persecuted specialist. A little divinity was taught, via the Greek Testament. Nothing else was.

The doors opened at seven in summer and eight in winter. There were boys hanging around the gate well before then. Cooper (the boys' favourite and the most sparing with the cane) was the only master who was strictly punctual; Sleath's own hours were very variable, and so was the time of morning prayers. The boys all brought bits of candle, which still had to be wax, in winter. These could not be lit until one of the masters' candles arrived; the dim building then lit up like an Easter Vigil, though often with mishaps contrived by the boys. The heating did little good, except in the first-formers' corner. You could, if your parents paid for it, have breakfast, at half-past eight, in one of the masters' houses. It was quite a good breakfast. If you brought your own, you could eat it in the schoolroom, which was supervised by a master, or you might prefer the unsupervised playground; but there you needed to be robust. Kingdon, the Jesuit, remembered the bullying with horror; but Chilton Mewburn, later a naval officer, enjoyed the 'rough and ready way of dealing out justice to cowards, bullies, or boys detected in "mean tricks"', which was to swing them by the hands and feet and bump them against stone pillars.

On Mondays, Wednesdays and Fridays there was another break, for dinner,

*'Beetles', in honour of distinguished Old Boys, have adorned the walls of the School since the early part of the nineteenth century.*

A

CATALOGUE

OF THE

𝔏𝔦𝔟𝔯𝔞𝔯𝔶

OF

ST. PAUL'S SCHOOL.

LONDON:

M.DCCC.XXXVI.
[NOT PUBLISHED.]

*In early times the Poor Scholar may have acted as Librarian. The first printed catalogue was made in 1743, one of the few achievements of Charles's High Mastership. This is Jowett's catalogue (1836).*

*Benjamin Jowett, by 'Spy'. (Vanity Fair, 9 April 1887).*

which lasted officially from eleven until one: but masters were often late in returning, and the schoolroom was a dangerous place for the smaller boys in the long high noon. Most boys went home for dinner: some ate at a master's house. Afternoon school ended at four. Tuesdays, Thursdays and Saturdays were half-holidays, when, unless rounded up for mathematics, everybody went home at twelve.

Seen in context, St Paul's was not a particularly violent or unruly school. In 1783, five eighth-formers were reported to the Governors for 'very disorderly and riotous behaviour'. Two were expelled, but one of these later apologized and was reinstated. Four of the five went on to Oxford or Cambridge, and two were eventually ordained. Barham remembers his friend Diggle, later a general, noisily interrupting a Quaker meeting and stealing a master's shoelaces. Kingdon knew a story that Barham's nephew, when Captain of the School, led a battle against Merchant Taylors', and was 'arrested with a drawn sword in his hand, taken before a magistrate, and dismissed with an admonition'. The fights with Merchant Taylors' (called 'stitch-lice' by the Paulines) were probably real enough, though the younger Barham, unlike his uncle, was never Captain of the School. The terrible 'Whack' himself, it is said, used to be greeted daily by the boys shouting in chorus 'Whack! row-de-dow!' But, even if true, all this is small beer compared to the violence and disorder at other public schools. In 1802 the Governors congratulated the boys on their spirited celebrations of the Peace of Amiens, and refunded their expenses. Although in 1806 one schoolmaster thought that out of Eton boys, Westminsters and Paulines, 'those of St. Paul's are the most depraved of all', nothing at St Paul's compared with the horrors of Long Chamber at Eton. Troops did not have to be called in, as they did at Winchester in 1818. St Paul's, after all, remained quite a small school for most of the nineteenth century, and the boarders, who caused most of the trouble, were getting fewer, and disappeared completely in Kynaston's time. He believed their removal had much improved the morals of the School: there had been a danger of 'boys passing through the playground at night and talking through the bars to loose women'.

Ballantine did not think that any of his contemporaries at St Paul's had achieved much distinction. Joseph Blakesley, Dean of Lincoln and Master of the Mercers' Company, who joined the School three weeks before Ballantine, could reasonably have objected to this dismissive observation. Another future Master, John Watney, was admitted in 1816, as was a rare Pauline aristocrat, Lucius Bentinck Cary, Viscount Falkland, later Captain of the Yeomen of the Guard and Governor of Bombay. This is, perhaps, only moderate distinction: but ten years after Ballantine there came to St Paul's a boy who was to epitomize its educational ideals as well as deeply influencing its future. He was Benjamin Jowett, the twelve-year-old son of a Fleet Street printer.

Perhaps the quintessential Victorian Sage, Jowett began as a schoolboy prodigy. Bookish from the first, he was frail, feminine in appearance and slight, even when Captain of the School. He was learned enough to be able, and poor enough to need, to catalogue the School Library before he went to Oxford. The Governors published the catalogue and paid him a hundred guineas. His kindness was so well known that the junior boys would regularly persuade him to do their translations – 'I say Jowett, give us a con there's a good fellow' – just as, years later, when

Professor of Greek, he would read and criticize the work of any undergraduate who cared to drop in on him. Before he left St Paul's, he knew most of Virgil and Sophocles by heart. Sleath thought him 'the best Latin scholar he had ever sent to college', and some of his early Greek verses are preserved in the School's 'Play-Book', a collection of work that had pleased the High Master enough to earn the School a half-holiday. When, in December 1836, he came back to St Paul's in triumph with the Balliol Scholarship, 'we boys held up our heads an inch or two higher than we did before', remembered C. R. Alford (later a bishop in Canada and Hong Kong). 'It was a sight worth beholding to gaze on the beaming countenance of our dear old High Master, Dr. Sleath.'

In 1836, Thomas Hughes was fourteen, so at about the same time that Jowett returned to St Paul's with the Balliol Scholarship, Old Brooke was ludicrously declaring, at the Rugby of Hughes's inventive memory, 'I know I'd sooner win two School-house matches running than get the Balliol Scholarship any day.' Young Jowett and Old Brooke are pointers: of course the age of athleticism really comes later, and of course St Paul's will not be exempt. Its independence of Arnoldian, and pseudo-Arnoldian, influences is neither absolute nor unique. But Jowett's was another spirit, older and, for many decades yet, more powerful.

Like Colet, Jowett made his name by his work on St Paul. Like Colet, he was persecuted, not very severely, for heresy. Like Colet's, too, were his educational generosity and vision. Devoted to the classics, he wanted them to be as widely studied and loved as possible; and here his known policy at Oxford relates to understanding the political struggle soon to burst on St Paul's. His success was the first glint of a dazzling century for his old School, which was 'at that time', wrote another Balliol Scholar of Jowett's day, 'not of very high classical repute'. It was not going to be possible to say that again. 'I do not profess to be a good scholar,' said Sleath, 'but I make my scholars polish one another.' Under Roberts fewer than ten per cent of Paulines, under Sleath more than twenty-five per cent, went on to the universities.

*Father Ignatius, by 'Ape'. (*Vanity Fair, *9 April 1897).*

It is almost as fashionable, and perhaps with equal justice, to blame the classical curriculum of Victorian schools for the decline of the British economy as it is to blame public school athleticism for the rise, or at any rate the management, of the British Empire. Jowett's classicism was neither dry nor mechanical, but attempted again the ideal synthesis of Erasmus's vision. Not that Colet's St Paul, or even Erasmus's Socrates, would have been at home with Jowett's. But the centre held: Jowett received, adorned and raised up a living tradition. There was more to Sleath's St Paul's than dust and tyranny and Greek verbs in coloured inks.

A recent novel of A. N. Wilson's uses Jowett to personify one horn of the Victorian religious dilemma, and Father Ignatius Lyne, 'the mad monk of Llanthony', the other. The odd irony that both these men were Paulines seems to have escaped him. Ignatius, who struggled for years, and with almost total failure, to establish an Anglican Benedictine monastery in the Black Mountains, was at St Paul's under Sleath's successor, Herbert Kynaston, who, after five years as Tutor at Christ Church, became High Master in 1838 at the age of twenty-eight.

'A more polished scholar and a worse disciplinarian there could not well be'; 'A ripe and very elegant classical scholar'; 'Kynaston was never a good schoolmaster' – there is virtual unanimity that Kynaston was kindly, charming, urbane and almost completely ineffectual. 'Why, my dear boy,' he exclaimed on being handed an imposition, 'I never intended you to do it!' He did not make an impressive showing before the Public Schools Commissioners in 1862; their report referred to a decline in academic performance since the 'palmy' time of Sleath. He did little to protect the unfortunate French master from his pupils. In his later years at least, the eighth-formers, whom he taught himself, could do as much or as little work as they pleased. They could also keep very lax hours, and Kynaston's own attendance was erratic. He liked to make a big show of Apposition, for which he wrote a great deal of verse, in Latin and English, for his pupils to recite. It is historical and religious, celebrating, with much ingenious oblique allusion, the history, especially the Christian history, of the School. The apogee of this was his *Lays of the Seven Half-Centuries* presented in 1859. 'So sit down, if you please, young gentlemen', Kynaston concluded his introductory speech, 'and our Dissolving Views shall immediately commence.'

Kynaston's scholarship was solid enough, no doubt, and whatever his shortcomings, he could inspire scholarship in those of his pupils capable of it. One such pupil, R. P. Brown, who himself became a headmaster, recognized both the weaknesses and the elusive powers which transcended them.

*Erasmus dedicated his* De Copia *(1512) to Colet: 'I thought it my duty to bestow some small literary present to assist in the furniture of your school.' This copy (Froben, Basel, 1536) was given by Kynaston to the School Library.*

There must ultimately have been a stimulus in Kynaston himself that made for scholarship. It was not teaching power; it was not disciplinary control; it was not exactly spiritual force. It was rather the personal ideal he exhibited in manners and in learning. He was felt to be *fide et literis* himself a model Pauline, the finished article, the fair copy of a gentleman and scholar.

For a moment, the distance from Arnold as perceived by his disciples is not so great, but Kynaston seems wholly to have lacked Arnold's stern conviction of the sinfulness of 'boy nature'. 'My dear boys' was often the only audible phrase in his addresses; he and his wife used to invite one or two of the worse-off boys to stay with them in the country in the summer; and he treated the eighth-formers with the gentleness due to small children while discussing Sophocles with them as though they were his scholarly equals.

By the 1870s Kynaston's ill-health had compounded his weaknesses: he had a horror of draughts. Yet, as Brown points out, these were years of glittering success for Paulines recently gone up to the universities. Through Kynaston's long High Mastership the School was permanently full, and the number of boys going on to the universities rose from twenty-five to thirty per cent. This was partly because parents of the established professions – clergy, lawyers, army officers, doctors,

*Mr Gladstone was among those present at Apposition in 1843. The speeches and recitations, in Latin, Greek and English, lasted two hours.*

together with a sprinkling of 'gentlemen' and merchants – almost completely displaced the humbler families who had previously patronized the School: but that in itself is an indication, at a time of revival of the other old public schools and the foundation of scores of new ones, of remarkable success. This is not to say that the conventional picture of Kynaston is a dissolving view, only that it poses a problem.

It is true that St Paul's probably benefited from the poor state of health of the other *London* public schools in the mid-nineteenth century; true too that the change of clientele probably partly resulted from the rapid disappearance of a resident lower middle class from the City. Yet this could have left the School empty rather than socially elevated. There must surely have been a positive side to Kynaston's regime, and more to it than just an ability to instil classical scholarship, still admittedly a royal road to a wide range of professional successes, into a select band of clever boys.

Indeed there was. The changes in school life brought about by, or at any rate under, Kynaston were remarkable. The evidence for them is obvious; it has been overshadowed by the dramatic events which followed so quickly, and the dramatic personality of his successor, whose achievements appeared more dramatic still when given as a back-cloth an 'age of decadence' rather than one of valuable if undramatic change. Kynaston seems to have been a real agent of curricular change, and not just the benign fainéant that he appears in his pupils' memoirs.

In 1838 there were still only four masters, James Cooper, the Third Master, having also taught mathematics since 1835. From 1843 a separate mathematician was employed, and from 1853 two French masters. Kynaston wanted to introduce German too, but did not manage to. By 1862 the junior boys, who did not do French, had a little history and geography (perhaps only ancient history and geography) with the High Master. From 1868 there was also a 'supernumerary Instructor in Composition and Extra Reading'. This was an extra, visiting, classics master, appointed for two years only. The post, which did not last beyond Kynaston's time, was held by some distinguished men. All of them Fellows of Oxford or Cambridge Colleges, they included W. R. Kennedy and A. W. Verrall. Thus, on paper, the staff had been doubled, though only the four previously existing masterships were full-time. Kynaston pressed the Governors to appoint a fifth full-time master, but they would not do so.

French and mathematics cannot be said to have had an entirely happy start. They were taught on half-holiday afternoons; turning the polite fiction that this was the purpose of the half-holidays into partial fact was not likely to make them popular. The first French masters were a Frenchman and an Italian. Monsieur Delille made the rounds, teaching at three other schools besides St Paul's, and made a good thing of it. He stood no nonsense. But Signor Tito Pagliardini was unfortunately the comic French master of the school story. From 1859, when he succeeded Delille as senior French master, 'French afternoon' was a time of uproarious misrule. Two masters, with the ineffectual help of two eighth-form monitors, were left to cope with a hundred or more boys. 'Distraction was cultivated by every means ... clockwork mice and other mechanical wonders, squeaking dolls ... and all kinds of music – and only weariness brought a respite from fooling.'

*Tito Pagliardini, French master from 1858 until 1878. He was 'enthusiastic in his profession, but quite unable to cope with the average English boy'.*

Pagliardini's life must have been wretched: his classes seem much less funny when one reflects on his enduring twenty years of them.

Mathematics was not at first taught below the fifth form. It had some similar early problems, at the heart of which was that only the classics were taken really seriously and affected a boy's promotion and prospects, and probably too that classics masters enjoyed a superior and more secure status and that this was not invisible to the boys. Mathematics, however, did have some standing at the universities; it was taught partly by the regular masters, and though the first master appointed specifically to teach mathematics (in 1843) was a failure, the second, William Lethbridge, was both a Wrangler and an able and inspiring schoolmaster, and the School's mathematics was singled out for praise by the Commissioners in 1862. Yet he had no control over the mathematics teaching of the other masters. No science was taught in Kynaston's time. One of Sleath's pupils, Alfred Smee, and one of Kynaston's, Edwin Ray Lankester, became distinguished scientists. Lankester, who had a good opinion of his own powers and T. H. Huxley as a family friend, was glad he got no science at school: 'probably it would have taken me many years to get over the evil influence of an incompetent science-schoolmaster'. He was grateful to Kynaston for allowing him to go off to science lectures in school time and for encouraging him to move on early to Cambridge.

Other school activities began to make an informal appearance. The Union Debating Society was founded by some eighth-formers in 1853. Kynaston soon allowed it to meet in the Library. A Music Society began in 1859: the boys elected

*Detail of an Edwin Ray Lankester cartoon from* Punch, *1905.*

*This engraving of the third school was published in 1827, three years after it was built. The east end of the Cathedral is on the extreme left.*

Opposite: *High Master Kynaston in 1855. To celebrate Apposition that year, Kynaston published* The Number of the Fish, a Lay on the Foundation *of St Paul's School.*

Right: *Sleath enthroned in the third School. The chair, and bust of Colet, are authentic enough, but the view of the Cathedral has perhaps been improved by artist's licence. 'Now and then the High Master would say to the Captain just before the end of morning school-time, "Fetch the playbook". Then we knew we were in for a half-holiday.'*

Overleaf, top: *R. J. Walker, the High Master's son, presented this window to Hammersmith Borough; it can still be seen in the reference library. Walker, who won the Hertford, Craven and Ireland Scholarships at Oxford, and inherited a large private fortune from his mother's father, considered buying a school when he was not elected High Master of St Paul's in 1905, but instead took to travel, book-collecting and scholarly publication. The arms on the right are Walker's. (Reproduced by courtesy of Hammersmith & Fulham Archives.)*

Overleaf, below: *Architect's drawing for the fourth School building. Waterhouse was immensely punctilious, and his minutely planned and executed drawings were part of the secret of his professional success. (Mercers' Company, London.)*

Below: *Rudolf Ackermann's* History of the Colleges . . . and Schools, *which appeared in 1816, contained these two prints of St Paul's. The interior is by Augustus Pugin the elder. The building, says the (anonymous) text, is uniform, and in a more advantageous situation, would attract attention as an example of elegant architecture.'*

the conductor, and rejected the candidature of Mr Kempthorne, the Surmaster, but at the first Annual Concert the following year, Kempthorne was the conductor, the principal pianist and a vocal soloist. The unfortunate Pagliardini also had a memorable singing voice. Some time after 1864 the Society – not the School – employed a music teacher. By 1877 the boys were giving a ball after the annual concert; the Governors objected. In 1861 came the foundation of an Athletic Sports Club, whose first meetings (for running, jumping and throwing the cricket ball) were held in Battersea Park. Mr Hudson, the Fourth Master, was president, and the versatile Mr Kempthorne was umpire. But there had been some, more or less organized, games by the end of the 1840s, cricket and rackets on Copenhagen Fields in north London, rowing on the Thames or the Lea, and a local fives, played without gloves, in the playground if it was not too foggy. All was quite voluntary. Among the earliest school cricket matches, those against Merchant Taylors' raised the most excitement, handed on, perhaps, from the earlier pitched battles. By 1866 there was a football club. At that date the local rules, though approximately Rugbeian, ordered that goals must be kicked 'underneath the goal rope'. Five years later the club was a foundation member of the Rugby Football Union.

It was Kynaston who, in 1858, suggested that a more easily accessible cricket ground could be acquired by renting part of Kennington Oval. He also actively

*In 1911, the Reverend Samuel Wetherfield, who had left St Paul's in 1861, wrote that modern Paulines 'little knew the efforts we had to make to get any cricket at all'. 'The Bedford Match – How's that?' is one of ten scenes drawn by Bertram Gilbert at the beginning of the twentieth century.*

promoted the creation of classrooms out of rooms in his own house and the shortening of school hours, which by 1862 lasted from nine until one and from two until four. This balanced the loss of one of the three half-holidays. By then, boarders, whose number had been declining, had disappeared, apart from a few who boarded with neighbours of the School by private arrangement. The later start in the day, as well as the coming of the underground railways, facilitated the growing intake of day boys from distant parts of London and beyond. When there was a public execution, school started an hour late, to avoid the crowds.

An anonymous but elderly old boy, writing in *The Pauline* in 1888 as 'Nemo', recalls his father bringing him to school on his first day. Dr Kynaston 'received us with a genial kindness that he never ceased to manifest, and which quite set me at ease'. He explained the need to bring a wax candle, 'solemnly read the rules' and 'studied my certificate of baptism'. Although by 1893 the old Pauline judge, Sir Charles Pollock, was maintaining, quite wrongly, that Colet had intended St Paul's for boys 'without distinction . . . of creed', it was Kynaston's regular practice to insist on a baptismal certificate, as had been ordered by the Governors in 1798. It was a rule that must have disappeared very quickly after his time, as Jewish boys were being sent to St Paul's on the eve of the move from the City. But Nonconformists and Roman Catholics were not excluded, though they may have been rare in Kynaston's time. Earlier, in 1786 and 1817, for instance, dissenting ministers' sons were admitted. Kynaston occasionally prepared boys for confirmation.

Kynaston must have been gratified by the presence, at Apposition in 1864, of the Prince of Wales, as well as two Archbishops, five bishops and an Old Pauline former Lord Chancellor. The Prince had lunch in the playground under the schoolroom, which had been 'tastefully decorated for the occasion', a Herculean task, surely. An ode by Kynaston was sung; its theme was *Doce, Disce aut Discede*, a motto which hung in the schoolroom for centuries, and which a slightly earlier generation of Paulines used to mistranslate: '*Doce*, flog the boys; *disce*, make the blood run; *aut*, or *discede*, turn them out of doors!' At the end of the ceremony, the Prince asked for a remedy, and was refused: only a reigning sovereign or a bishop, present in the School, might do so, according to the Statutes. Then all seven prelates rose in turn and asked for one, and a week's holiday was granted. This was just the kind of drama that the High Master enjoyed; presumably he briefed all the great men carefully in advance, though one boy who was present thought the Prince was surprised and annoyed. A little over a century later, when an Old Pauline archbishop spontaneously asked for a remedy, the Surmaster made sure he did not get it: there were holidays enough, he thought, and the request had been made in the Cathedral, not, as directed by the Statutes, in the School.

Not long afterwards, the Prince of Wales voted against the Governors of St Paul's School in the House of Lords. He was Chairman of a Committee dealing with the recommendations of a Royal Commission, led by the Earl of Clarendon, which was set up in 1861 to investigate the nine 'great public schools', of which St Paul's was one. There was a wide range of reasons for public unease about the schools. Like the ancient universities, to which many of their pupils went on, they were under pressure to reform their curricula to meet the needs of a consciously vigorous and expanding country. They were challenged both by the reform of Arnold, paralleled or imitated in some but not all of them, and by the astonishing success of such new schools as Wellington and Marlborough. Some of them – and here St Paul's was conspicuous – were believed to have large endowments which might not be being put to adequate use. A few years earlier there had been scandalous exposures of such endowments being diverted at Dulwich and the King's School, Rochester. The Mercers themselves were attacked in the House of Lords over the management of their hospital at Greenwich.

As Governors of St Paul's School, the Mercers could certainly not be accused of negligence. In an earlier investigation, the Charity Commissioners set up in 1818 had on the whole reported favourably, stating themselves satisfied that the funds were 'honourably applied'. They had, however, criticized the scale of the Apposition Dinner, which at £229 9s. 6d. cost only £50 less than the Usher's annual salary. The commissioners also found the annual gift of a medal (now gold with a value of £20) to the Surveyor Accountant 'hard to justify'. More serious was their statement that the large revenue of the Trust could, 'under a somewhat more economical management', be put to much greater beneficial use than was provided by the existing School. Thus the Mercers, despite improvements over

*The Prince of Wales at Apposition, 15 June 1864. Though the Prince became a father, and Chairman of the Governors of Wellington College, that same year, the Queen wrote a few days later that he 'has the best intentions, but is not discreet'. Kynaston is on the extreme left, with hand raised. The Surveyor Accountant of the Mercers' Company is presenting the prizes.*

the forty years following, may have met the Clarendon Commission with some apprehension, and were relieved to be able, despite the Prince's vote, to escape from the provisions of the Public Schools Act of 1866, on a legal technicality. Merchant Taylors' also escaped, for similar reasons. This had the effect of separating the two day schools from the other seven in the public mind at a time when boarding education was becoming increasingly fashionable, all of which helped produce a certain touchiness in St Paul's in the second half of the century. Moreover, exclusion from the Public Schools Act brought St Paul's into the scope of the more radical and formidable Endowed Schools Commissioners and, from 1874, their successors, the now permanent Charity Commissioners. With these bodies the Governors fought an ultimately successful Thirty Years' War. With hindsight, they came to wish that they had not been so anxious to shrug off the comparatively easy yoke of the Public Schools Commission, but the final irony is that the view that this automatically handed them over to the Endowed Schools Commissioners, unexpected, unwelcome and yet unquestioned at first, was probably a legal mistake.

The moderation of the Public Schools Commission was, in any case, only relative. On 2 July 1862, they visited the School and interviewed first five members of the Court of Assistants and then the High Master in the Library. They asked

*Samuel Walker, an Old Pauline professional photographer, took this view of the schoolroom in 1876. The windows on the Cathedral (left) side were double-sashed to keep out the noise.*

some awkward questions. The Governors were pressed hard about their claims over the Colet Trust. Their position was that, though they would never use its funds for anything but the benefit of the School, they were absolute owners of any surplus to the School's requirements under the Statutes. They could show that they had, in fact, provided well beyond those requirements. Still, there was a huge surplus, which would grow much bigger before the end of the century; and yet the School still had only 153 boys, cramped surroundings and a squalid playground.

Ought St Paul's to move? It was clear that there was no other solution to the problem of its inadequate facilities and numbers. There was confusion about whether Colet had laid down that it was for Londoners. The High Master asserted that this was stated in the Statutes: he was wrong, though Colet does mention his special concern for the education of Londoners elsewhere. Kynaston was also confused about his own wishes: at first he is firmly against a move of any kind; later he seems quite enthusiastic at proposals to buy a country site, Haileybury College. (He was unaware that it had already been acquired for a new school, whose headmaster had been appointed a few days previously.) In any case, a move, whether to the country, the suburbs, or another part of London, was firmly opposed by a majority of the Governors present, though it had been recommended by two committees appointed by the Court of Assistants in 1859–60.

Prominent among the members of the second of these committees was the Reverend Joseph Blakesley. A former Master of the Mercers and future Dean of Lincoln, Blakesley might have become High Master himself in 1838 instead of Kynaston, but, though of a family long prominent in the Company, he objected to the thraldom in which the Court of Assistants still kept the High Master. He now showed his disagreement with his colleagues plainly enough to be called back, later in the year, for a further interview. He revealed that he had pressed for the purchase of Haileybury, while it had been on the market, not for the existing School to move to, but as an additional boarding school, whose boys should be charged the cost of their boarding. Blakesley was a distinguished scholar, whose 'kingly intellect' and 'subtle wit' were praised by the youthful Tennyson. A former Captain of the School, his testimony was more impressive, both for historical grasp and for vision, than either the High Master's or his fellow Governors'. He would not send his own sons to St Paul's while it stayed on its existing site.

The Commissioners thought Blakesley's new country school would kill its elder sister and, though he denied that this was the intention, perhaps he would not have much minded. The plan for a second school, scotched for the time being, did not die. But Blakesley's percipience is clearest in his isolation of the two major obstacles to any substantial change. One was a stubborn inertia, born partly from caution and partly from jealousy of proprietary claims, which prevented any really enterprising use of surplus revenue: 'I do not think that the necessity of doing anything with the surplus presses very strongly on their imagination.' 'They merely let them accumulate?' 'Yes.' The other was patronage.

Although in 1808 the Governors had restored to the High Master the power to place boys in the form he thought fit, they retained the right of admission to the School themselves. Until 1824 this right was in the hands of the Surveyor Accountant. From 1824, members of the Court of Assistants took it in turns to

*The Library in the third School had originally been part of the High Master's house. Kynaston allowed senior boys to study there, and often retreated there himself in cold weather. The Cathedral can just be seen through the windows.*

nominate boys, with the Surveyor Accountant and his Assistant and successor retaining two nominations for themselves. Kynaston was allowed to nominate one boy a year himself, as a privilege. He could reject boys as unsuitable, if the Governors agreed, but it was awkward for him to do so: the only test on admission was one of basic literacy. From 1814 no boys except the 153 Foundationers had been admitted, perhaps because the admission of others was seen as a back door to the Foundation, to which many of them did later proceed. One of Kynaston's answers seems to be hinting that the Court of Assistants feared that to expand the School would dilute the value of their patronage.

> It is very difficult to get in, because people, knowing that there is no payment made, the gentlemen who possess nominations are very much beset by applications, and they give them away to their own friends. There is great difficulty found in obtaining nominations, if a person does not choose to place himself under an obligation, or to take so much trouble.

A place at St Paul's was valuable also because of the leaving exhibitions tenable at the universities. One of them was now worth over £100 a year – too much, some of the Commissioners thought. Almost any reasonably respectable eighth-former could get one, and evidence was produced to show that Paulines at Oxford and Cambridge were not so well read as other public school boys. There was no means of superannuation, though the examiners had asked for one as early as 1822: in the fourth form there was a boy of fifteen whose work was worse than that of another aged eleven. Blakesley thought this was bound to do moral harm, as well as mental. He wanted, as he put it, to 'sweep out the drones'.

Giving evidence before the Commission must have been an ordeal; even so, the witnesses revealed some surprising gaps in their knowledge. The Master of the Mercers could not give the date of Kynaston's most recent salary increase and seemed not to know when he had succeeded Sleath. Kynaston was wrong in thinking that very few of his boys lived in the City, and boasted of a quite fictitious Old Pauline, the first Lord Angelsea, Councillor to Henry VIII. He had to admit to having very little idea of what the boys did in their dinner-hours: the Governors accepted no responsibility for it. Even Blakesley was wrong in thinking that 'the bulk' of the boys' fathers were clergymen. Almost exactly a third were.

When the Commissioners raised, once again, the cost of the Apposition dinner, they received in reply an invitation to the next one. Whether or not they accepted, their recommendations for St Paul's were unpalatable: they described the admissions system as 'vicious' and referred to 'langour and stagnancy' in some parts of the School. They wanted the High Master to be given back the power to appoint other masters; they wanted science, music and drawing introduced. They suggested considerable expansion and a move to a larger site in the north-west of London. Most important, in the Commissioners' own view, were their proposals for changing the governing body, which they wanted to be smaller, and to include an equal number of Mercers and Crown nominees.

It is hard to see why McDonnell thought that the School could congratulate itself on its escape from the Clarendon Commission. Sooner or later, all its proposals, except the alterations to the Governors, were implemented, though the move, twenty years later, was to the west rather than the north-west. In 1870 legal judgement was given against the Mercers' claim to outright ownership of the Colet estate; they held it 'entirely for the use and benefit of the School as a Charity'. All plans now had to be made in the distorting shadow of the long struggle with the Charity Commissioners.

Critical as they were in many ways, the Public Schools Commissioners did not disapprove of the essentially classical education provided by St Paul's, nor of its being provided mainly for the upper middle classes. The Charity Commissioners, and considerable pressure groups in London, were now to call in question the value of what was provided, and the justice of providing it for an exclusive clientele. The London County Council (LCC) later sought representation on the governing body, and the Fulham Vestry, or parish council of the area into which the School moved during the debate, pressed for its funds to be made available for a wide range of local education. Against them was soon ranged an apparently almost unanimous phalanx of Governors, masters and Old Paulines, loudly supported by *The Times*. These defenders of what seemed to themselves the status quo won an almost complete victory in the end (1900). By then they were defending the Clarendon Commissioners' rejected model, not the school which those Commissioners had criticized.

The Endowed Schools Commissioners and their successors, the Charity Commissioners, had extensive statutory powers of reorganization which they exercised with vigour. There were, however, legal safeguards for those whose interests were

*The Prince of Wales's wedding procession passed the School and turned right towards the west door of the Cathedral on 7 March 1863. The School claimed the privilege of presenting a loyal address when a king or queen passed by: on this occasion the address was displayed outside the building and presented later at Buckingham Palace.*

involved. Most of the schools that the Commissioners dealt with put up little resistance; they lacked powerful friends and the money and legal experience that the Worshipful Company of Mercers could bring to bear. At Apposition in 1893 the Old Pauline Master, Colonel Clementi, spoke of the Commissioners with anger and contempt, as 'deeply imbued with the traditions of the most narrow-minded period of English history', and issuing stereotyped schemes 'which could be reproduced for any school by a clerk in a couple of days. If St. Paul's', he went on with arrogant irony, 'does not happen to be a country grammar school, so much the worse for St. Paul's.'

The pride with which Clementi spoke is one clue to the eventual victory of his party. They certainly owed much to skilful legal footwork; they owed more to changes in the School so spectacularly successful as to make it hard to criticize – and these changes implemented some of the proposals made by the very Charity Commissioners who were now the Enemy. But only some of the proposals; others were delayed, or side-stepped, or misunderstood, perhaps accidentally-on-purpose, or just brazenly ignored. A recent writer, full of hostility to what he sees as the class prejudices of the victors, cannot withhold his admiration for this 'resourceful' and 'determined' campaign, as he describes their attacker 'baulked of its prey by the stubborn St Paul's defenders', moving on 'to easier game'.

The Commissioners' proposal, made in 1874, that the School should move from the City, was neither unwelcome nor, of course, new. An alteration in the governing body was also accepted without much difficulty in 1876: from that date it has consisted of the Master and Wardens of the Mercers, nine nominees of the Court of Assistants and three representatives each of the universities of Oxford, Cambridge and London. The Company retains the management of the Colet estate. The Court of Assistants also abandoned their right to nominate boys for admission. The first entrance scholarship examination was held in January 1877. In September 1876, six boys were admitted as 'Capitation Scholars', so-called because the High Master received fees for them by the head. These were the first such for over half a century. From this date on, regular admissions only took place at the beginning of each term, instead of whenever there was a vacancy. The Mercers also gave up the annual dismissal and reappointment of the statutory masters, and allowed the High Master to appoint his assistants.

Thus they cleared the decks for the real battle. The proposals which the School authorities found seriously objectionable were: governors nominated by the LCC and other local boards; a proportion of the scholarships to be restricted to boys from the cheaper endowed schools and from elementary (or 'board') schools; the foundation of a new 'modern' school independent of St Paul's but paid for out of its endowments, or of a separate modern department within St Paul's School with a right to a proportion of the scholarships; and a legal restriction on the annual expenditure of the Colet estate on St Paul's School itself. The Commissioners did not press for all these all the time, nor did the defenders hold a consistent line. On one other major proposal they gave way, despite the strong feelings of Colonel Clementi: this was the foundation of a girls' school, accepted in principle in 1876, but only opened in 1904.

The tactics of both sides in this long and complex dispute can be made to appear devious, and perhaps they were. Yet the frequent changes in personnel of the governing body on the one hand and the numerous and conflicting pressures on the Charity Commissioners on the other helped make complete consistency difficult. The Governors certainly felt that they were fighting for a coherent cause, and probably for a noble one, the integrity of the School, the ideals of the Founder, the highest standards of education. Their opponents then, and at least one historian since (G. Cannell in 1981), accused them of struggling for selfish class interests, and trying to keep the poor of London from any share in the benefits of Colet's generosity. Cannell writes of 'passionate determination to exclude lower class boys from the school at all costs'. On the other hand, R. C. Seaton, who became a master at St Paul's at the height of the struggle, wrote (in 1911) that 'St. Paul's is glad to welcome boys from any class provided they can profit by the education'.

'Provided they can profit by the education': for them to do so, the method of entry must not be designed to exclude them, and the curriculum must be one they could benefit from. To such radical critics as James Beal, member of the LCC for Fulham, who in 1894 published *St. Paul's School and its Scandals*, the School authorities were deliberately making it impossible for the poor, for whom it had been founded, to use it. The cases of Harrow and Rugby, which really were intended for the local poor, provided apparent parallels: Beal claimed to have discovered by examining early school lists that most of the boys originally came from the families of city tradesmen and shopkeepers. But no such lists exist; Beal's opponents could easily show that, apart from the one poor scholar, Colet's School was not founded for the poor any more than for the rich. It was, however, certainly not founded exclusively for the rich: the introduction of competitive examinations, more or less impossible to pass without the right kind of primary education, and the foundation of a preparatory school, with substantial fees, by an assistant master at St Paul's, looked to Beal and his allies like a class conspiracy.

It is unlikely, in a period when education and social class were as sensitively and intimately entwined as ever in English history, that there was nobody among the defenders of St Paul's with some snobbish motivation. Thus in 1875 the Reverend Mr Whittington moved a resolution which declared that, by the plans of the Commissioners, St Paul's, 'one of the nine public schools of England, is now degraded to the level of a board school'. It is equally unlikely, however, that the main thrust of the defence was on social grounds disguised as educational. Two of the most influential defenders were Jowett (Vice-Chancellor of Oxford in 1892) and Sir Charles Pollock, a baron of the Exchequer. Jowett was the son of an unsuccessful and impoverished businessman, and, tuft-hunter though he was, his whole life bears witness to his hostility to educational exclusiveness based on class. Cannell is sarcastic about Pollock's contempt for working-class boys, but Pollock's father, Lord Chief Baron Pollock, also an Old Pauline, was the son of a saddler. His own success and his family's would have been blocked at its beginning by the social exclusiveness his son is alleged to have been seeking. It is quite true that, in practice, there were few Paulines of working- or even lower middle-class background at the School in the late nineteenth century – a search through the registers reveals a rare woollen warehouseman's son entering in 1891 – it may or may not be true, but it was certainly contended, that many of the professional families that did send their sons to the School would have been driven out by the cost of subsidizing the poor. (Whereas Beal claimed that only two boys who entered the School between 1870 and 1876 were orphans or sons of widows, there were in fact twenty-two.) Jowett and Pollock were not defending the middle classes from contamination by working-class boys, but the modified but still intact classical education, 'Godliness and good learning', among whose recent proponents had been the great Old Pauline headmaster of King Edward's Birmingham, James Prince Lee.

At Birmingham, Lee, who was an admired member of Arnold's staff at Rugby in the 1830s, had inspired extraordinary devotion in an extraordinary sixth form, which included a future Archbishop of Canterbury, as well as two of the greatest of English biblical scholars, B. F. Westcott and J. B. Lightfoot, successively bishops of Durham. Even the Clarendon Commissioners referred to Lee (by then Bishop of Manchester) with respect verging on awe (Kynaston wrongly told them that he had been a boarder). The teaching that so inspired his able pupils combined an enormous but discriminating involvement in classical literature with an almost grimly earnest, but equally learned, Christianity: at its heart was the Greek Testament. But he also expected wide and demanding reading outside the classics, and was no enemy to modern or scientific studies, so long as they knew their place. The effect of his work, and that of like-minded men at other schools, on the intelligentsia of the Victorian Christian establishment has been illuminatingly described by David Newsome. It was not simply Arnoldian, though Arnold was a major influence. It had hardly affected St Paul's directly yet, though it grew partly out of the Pauline Christian humanist soil, *fide et literis*, in which Lee had grown up.

Kynaston was not grim, and his earnestness was tempered by the balanced ele-

*Joseph Hurst Lupton, DD (1836–1905) was Surmaster for thirty-five years, Librarian, classicist, mathematician and historian. He gave a stained glass window to Wakefield Cathedral, and a drinking fountain to Brook Green. His 'speech and writing were both characterised by graceful dignity'.*

74

gance and reserve of the Westminster of an earlier age. (It is strange that one modern writer on Victorian headmasters should have taken him for a Wykehamist.) But Kynaston was nearly seventy; in his last years he left the management of the School almost entirely to the young Surmaster, J. H. Lupton. In 1876 he retired to his prebend of Holborn at St Paul's Cathedral and two years later he died. The man who was chosen to succeed him had been a boy at Rugby shortly after Arnold's death, and gone to Manchester as High Master of the Grammar School during Lee's episcopate there. He was as formidable as either, and utterly committed, whatever his reservations as to their religious ideals, to the defence of the essentially classical educational programme which they had successfully reinvigorated. Whether or not the Governors knew in 1876 that they had found a great High Master, they were quite aware that they were appointing a heavyweight champion.

*The last days of the old School building, about 1894, when it was soon to be pulled down. At a farewell gathering ten years earlier, Auld Lang Syne was sung 'with wondrous vigour' and 'scarcely anyone could have felt unmoved as he left the dear old place, never to enter it again'.*

# VII

## 'THE MAN FROM MANCHESTER'

*H. D. Elam on F. W. Walker*

### 1877–1905

*'Spy' cartoon of High Master Walker.*

FREDERICK WILLIAM WALKER was the son of an unsuccessful hatter from Northern Ireland, who claimed descent from a hero of the siege of Londonderry. It is probably not true that he worked in the Rugby hat shop which sold Tom Brown his first 'tile'. To have moved from Southwark, where his son attended the grammar school, to Rugby, for his son to become a day boy there, indicates that he still had middle-class means of a sort. At Oxford, where he was Scholar and then Fellow of Corpus, Walker won high honours in the schools, the Vinerian Scholarship in Law, and the Tancred Scholarship in Sanskrit, but lost his conventional Christian faith either then or soon afterwards, at just about the time when it was becoming not unconventional for clever young men to do so. Probably his inability to take Orders at a time when all the great headmasters were clergymen contributed to his hesitation about a career. He was called to the Bar, and only persuaded with great difficulty to accept the high mastership of Manchester Grammar School in 1859. He was still just under thirty.

Walker was influenced by the later Utilitarians and the early Positivists, but his pragmatic energy was all his own. 'The chief requisite for success is a determined will' is one of the many apophthegms attributed to him, and the most characteristic. He found Manchester Grammar School in what looked like terminal decline and

76

left it the most respected school in the north of England, with a wholly reformed curriculum, including physics and chemistry, 'subjects of which', says an historian of that school, 'he knew and cared little'. Though he refused the possible offer of two Oxford Chairs, it was not of his own choosing that he stayed in Manchester seventeen years: he had already sought the headmasterships of two London schools, Charterhouse in 1863 and King's College School in 1866. In 1867 he married the daughter of a wealthy Manchester Nonconformist who was also a governor of the school. She died two years later, leaving him financially independent. Whether or not his ambition contributed to his marital choice, his fearlessness antedates his marriage, and his single-minded, dynamic determination was perhaps fuelled further by his personal loss.

Walker had gained the friendship of Jowett while still at Oxford and retained it until Jowett's death in 1893. This is likely to have been the deciding factor in his appointment to St Paul's; the year before it an Old Pauline clergyman had attested publicly, without foundation but without contradiction, that the High Master had to be a clergyman. But of course Walker's achievement at Manchester strongly recommended him: he had won some battles there with local interests and with the Charity Commissioners, and he had built extensively. At St Paul's he would rout all the critics of the School, local and national, and rebuild entirely. From the first, he enjoyed the Governors' full confidence. They consulted him about everything, and almost always took his advice.

The move from the City was no longer in question by the time of Walker's appointment; it had been proposed by the Commissioners in 1874 and agreed upon by 1876. A committee of Governors met at Addison Road station, and walked over several sites in the neighbourhood. The place they chose (despite the objections of Westminster School) was about 16 acres, and cost £41,000. It was called Deadman's Fields, 'somewhere in the Western District' a conservative Old Boy called it scathingly, but West Kensington on the School's writing paper, and Hammersmith in common parlance. It was the largest step, metaphorically as well as literally, in the history of the School, but Walker did not wait to begin its transformation; his seven years in the City were years of rapid preparatory change.

The growth in numbers had begun a few months before Walker's arrival, with the admission of the first six Capitation Scholars in September 1876. The total number of boys rapidly rose to about 220. Walker did not move into the High Master's house, and the Surmaster vacated his: both were turned into classrooms; thus, even before the move, the old system of teaching all or nearly all the School in one great room had been given up. Two attics were allocated to the first science master, appointed in 1879; by 1884 he was somehow managing to teach fifty-four boys in the two science forms. The main schoolroom, now known as Hall, was still used for prayers. For the rest of the day it contained boys of different ages, chosen and taught by Walker, the group that came to be known as the Special.

Unlike earlier High Masters, Walker never taught the eighth form; after the move he had no form of his own. He is supposed to have told the Governors when they interviewed him that a headmaster's function was 'to walk about and hear everything'. He was thought Olympian in his remoteness, his rather awesome presence (he was a small man with a large beard and a large voice) and his occasional

frightening, if artificial, rages; yet there is a wealth of vivid anecdote about him which suggests affection and even intimacy with some of the boys and their families – more, perhaps, than with his assistant masters. The numbers of these he at once increased: there were thirteen altogether on the eve of the move, eight classicists including the High Master, one French master (a temporary reduction), two mathematicians, a scientist and the first art master, Robert Harris, who was also obliged to teach geometry. Thus Walker had staff enough to be himself supervisory, strategical and circumambient. One of his staff praised him for his trust in his assistant masters and 'his manner of leaving them alone', but this was selective – there are stories enough about his unexpected and disconcerting appearances in classrooms to give point to part of another epigram that perhaps he coined: 'Boys are always reasonable, masters sometimes, parents never.'

In fact, though Walker was quick to remove the existing French and mathematics masters, he inherited an able, even an outstanding, staff. J. H. Lupton, Surmaster from 1866 to 1899, editor and biographer of Colet, preacher to Gray's Inn and Hulseian Lecturer in 1877, was also the subject of one of the earliest clerihews ('Praise the Lord for his mercies! I never did his Latin verses'). His successor as Surmaster, J. W. Shepard, who was on the staff of St Paul's from 1861 to 1902, was 'dear old Shepard' to Compton Mackenzie and the favourite uncle of E. H.

78

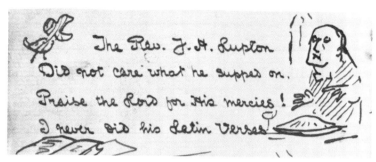

The earliest surviving clerihews were collected in an exercise book now in the School Library. E. C. Bentley, G. K. Chesterton and some of their friends all contributed, but Chesterton illustrated every verse. This one is by Bentley, whose identifying sign was the dodo. The collection was published by OUP in 1982 as The First Clerihews.

Shepard, the illustrator, though too short-sighted to recognize his nephew on the boy's first day at school. He was remembered for his good temper and early athletic enthusiasm, but also – a key quality in Walker's eyes – for his ability to spot a clever boy and bring him on. He was in turn succeeded by R. B. Gardiner, an Old Pauline who taught at St Paul's from 1875 to 1909, long enough to be able to describe himself as the Mercers' 'last surviving servant under Colet's Statutes'. He shared with Lupton a learned affection for the School's history and its Library: they were the first two masters to be librarians, rescued the Library from neglect and decay, and acquired a collection of early editions connected with Pauline history. Gardiner's two volumes of *Admissions Registers* (1884 and 1906), Lupton's *Life of Colet* (1887), and the *History of St Paul's School* (1909) by Michael McDonnell, who had only left the School in 1900, ensured that it was a very tradition-conscious St Paul's that put down its new roots in that remote 'Western District'.

Of fifteen masters appointed by Walker before the move, only five were still on his staff ten years later. W. G. Rutherford went on to be a famous headmaster of Westminster. Paul Blouet, a more than usually effective French master, lasted from 1877 to 1885; he had a legendary past in the Franco-Prussian war and a successful future (as Max O'Rell) writing about England through foreign eyes. Maurice Macmillan taught for six years at St Paul's before leaving to get married, join the family firm and become the father of the prime minister. (Ninety years later, another prime minister's son, Robin Wilson, taught at St Paul's for a spell.)

Above: *Alfred James Carver was a boy at St Paul's under Sleath, Surmaster from 1852 to 1858, and afterwards probably the greatest Master of Dulwich College. He visited St Paul's in his old age (c. 1893), and was sketched (left) with J. H. Lupton by a boy in the Lower Eighth, Gervaise Bailey.*

*Blouet/O'Rell (1848–1903) was impressed by the debating society at St Paul's, dedicated his edition of Dumas's* The Black Tulip *to the pupils of the Upper Eighth, and left his library to the School. He remarked, however, that in English public schools 'les crétins n'y sont pas méprises comme chez nous', and the title of one of his numerous popular books was* Drat the Boys.

Opposite: *Norman Wilkinson (d.1934) designed this poster for the London Midland and Scottish Railway in honour of its locomotive,* St Paul's School. *The School is here seen from the south-east, with the Great Hall in the background.*

Prominent among those who lasted longer were two men who came with Walker from Manchester. J. E. Melluish, a future Surmaster, had been on his staff there, and Samuel Bewsher had been the high master's secretary as well as teaching, and now took on the same post at St Paul's, becoming the first Bursar in 1884, when the distance from Mercers' Hall made the appointment necessary. Walker also persuaded him to found a preparatory school that would equip future Paulines with the right early education. This school began with six boys in the basement of Bewsher's own house in West Kensington three years before St Paul's moved. In 1890 it moved to new buildings opposite St Paul's in the Hammersmith Road. It had a new name, too, Colet Court, and more than three hundred boys. Bewsher's connection with Walker was regarded as corruptly close by the School's political enemies, and James Beal more than hinted that he used his official duties, which included the supervision of examinations, to the benefit of his pupils and as part of the grand object of excluding the poor. This was probably as false as the rumour of a subway under Hammersmith Road to link the two schools, but it is true that Bewsher was succeeded by his brother, James, an old MGS boy, as headmaster, and that their sister taught the smallest boys. James Bewsher, in defending his brother against charges of monopolizing entry to St Paul's, writes that, between 1884 and 1890, of 1179 boys admitted, 689 came from Bewsher's and 490 from other schools. In the 1920s new boys from Colet Court crossed the road in procession, while two policemen held up the traffic.

> On the far side, we looked back to wave farewell to Colet Court, and passed through the gates of St Paul's, onwards past Dean Colet's statue, to the steps of the School. Here we were greeted by the two Hall Porters, Spikey and Boss-eye. (It is worth recording that for all my time at St Paul's, I never learnt their real names.) These two sturdy fellows led us in procession up the steps and along the corridor leading to the Great Hall where we were, in turn, welcomed by Mr Pantin with a resounding 'Ave! Ave! New Boys!'

The architect of the new school buildings, Alfred Waterhouse, was chosen in 1878, defeating Gilbert Scott and Edward Barry. He was a man of sanguine energy comparable to the High Master's, and like him had made his name in Manchester, where he built the Assize Court, much of the University, and the new Town Hall, opened in 1877. He also rebuilt Balliol College, Oxford; Jowett regarded his work there as 'really beautiful'. But his masterpiece, completed at about the same time as he began work on the new St Paul's, was not much more than a mile away from it; the Natural History Musuem at South Kensington was opened in 1881, and much enjoyed by Compton Mackenzie when a thirteen-year-old Pauline fifteen years later (though more for the ichthyosaurus than for the architecture).

Waterhouse's work was controversial, both during and after his lifetime. Though a decided Gothicist, he was not doctrinaire stylistically, but gave first place to functional considerations, and made bold use of terracotta, brick and iron. His liking for symmetry and splendour of skyline was also evident in his St Paul's, which he hoped would have a 'sedate and scholastic appearance'. He was given what at first seemed a spacious site to work on, amid what was still more or less

# ST. PAUL'S SCHOOL

By NORMAN WILKINSON P.R.I.

St. Paul's School was founded in 1509 by John Colet, Dean of St. Paul's Cathedral and friend of
Erasmus and Sir Thomas More, for 153 boys 'of all nacions and countres indifferently, to be taught
free in the same,' and remained for nearly 400 years under the shadow of the great Cathedral.
In 1884 it moved to the present building at Hammersmith, the work of Alfred Waterhouse, and to-day
contains almost 800 boys.   Always a famous home of the Classics, it now devotes itself equally successfully
to History, Mathematics and Science; nor are games neglected, the School teams being prominent in
every branch of sport, with Boxing perhaps occupying the place of honour.   Famous Old Paulines of
the past include John Milton, Samuel Pepys, and the great Duke of Marlborough; among the most
distinguished of contemporary O.P.'s may be mentioned the late G. K. Chesterton and Compton Mackenzie,
in literature; the Rev. P. T. B. Clayton, Lord Dawson of Penn, Mr. P. G. H. Fender, Sir Otto Niemeyer,
the financial expert, and Mr. Eric Kennington.   The School's motto is 'Fide et Literis.'

FAMOUS PUBLIC SCHOOLS ON THE LMS

*Eric Kennington, war artist and portrait painter, left St Paul's the year before Hillard's High Mastership began, having won the prize for drawing three years running. Hillard admired this severe and perceptive portrait of himself enough to ask for a replica as a 'personal memorial'.*

*During 1989 the School's life was a sometimes disconcerting symbiosis with extensive and intensive building work – form rooms and offices suddenly became voids, and portacabins crowded the main quadrangle. Here, the emerging CDT blocks can be vaguely discerned in the centre.*

open country, fields and market gardens. The majestic, if rather stark, building he raised on it covered almost the whole northern side of the grounds, set back from the Hammersmith Road behind a grassed courtyard, planted with plane trees. On the southern side playing fields extended into what is now the centre of the Talgarth Road. At one end of the main building was placed a new house for the High Master; at the other already stood the Red Cow, a rustic public house. Together with the rest of the world, it was shut out by a wall of red brick, alternating with iron palings. Some of this still stands.

The same brick, dirt-resistant, hard and reddish-purple, was the principal material of the whole building and was the main complaint of those who disliked it. 'Indigestible in the carbolic red of its material', wrote a modern critic, and a contemporary spoke of Waterhouse going on to his next work 'with his hands still red from St. Paul's School'. At first it towered over a wilderness; Lupton remembered 'alluvial deposits suggestively prolific of thistles'. But buildings soon began to grow up round it and Virginia creeper over it. Though Pevsner thought that it had 'an odd inability to age gracefully', by the 1960s its northern front, seen through its trees from a bus in the Hammersmith Road, did not lack grace, and its southern front, from across its playing fields on a sunny morning outside Barons Court station, did not lack grandeur.

Grandeur was to be found inside, too. There were three main storeys with an attic floor above and a cloistered semi-subterranean floor below. This was intended to provide a covered playground, like the one in the City, and was later used for roller-skating, debates and the Tuck Shop. The Great Hall, too, was used at

*The original Library at Hammersmith, replaced by the Walker Library in 1913, was turned into the Chapel in 1926. The stained glass windows, all lost when the School moved to Barnes, depicted scenes from the life of Colet.*

first as the schoolroom had been in the last days at the City, not only for prayers for the whole school, but for the Special Class, formally named from 1885. The Board Room, at first called the Governors' Room, was intended as the successor to that room in the first building reserved for the Governors and examiners, the Apposing Chamber: in practice it served as a very large study for the High Master. At Walker's request, it was originally to have had a window on to the central Hall, and a view of the entrance to every classroom. He would be able to see all boys who came out 'and follow them with his eye to the door of the Retiring room'. Unlike the school in the City, the new St Paul's had a dining-hall, a lecture theatre, an art school and twenty-four custom-built classrooms, all facing north. There was no permanent chapel until 1926.

Although the proportions of the entrance hall, staircases and main rooms were generous (apart from the rather low rafters of the dining-hall) their decoration was at first austere, even institutionally dingy. Money was tight, the auction of the lease of the old site turning out a failure. But in all other respects the move was an immense success. Apposition was held at the City for the last time on 22 July 1884, and the following day the new buildings were opened by the Lord Chancellor and blessed by the Bishop of London. 'Better, better, much better', muttered Jowett.

Without troubling to count the bishops present, the Governors gave the boys an extra week's holiday, on the School Captain's request, so for them life at the new School began in the autumn term. There were then 211 of them; by 1888 there were 573. The new building was in theory designed for a thousand, and the Charity Commissioners at that time envisaged separate classical and modern departments for five hundred boys each, with a 'modern' headmaster, with some autonomy, under Walker. Although Waterhouse was well known for his skill in providing for his clients' practical needs, it soon became apparent to the Governors and the High Master that the buildings could not conveniently take more

*The west front of the School with the Red Cow, as seen from the Hammersmith Road, photographed about 1900.*

than six hundred, and around that figure the numbers stayed. 'I will have no democracy where I rule', Walker liked to say. Nor was there any doubt that, despite laboratories and within a few years a history eighth and specialist forms for would-be soldiers and doctors, the classics still ruled. Walker used the teaching of other subjects as evidence that a modern department existed; he never fully implemented the Commissioners' provisions about non-classical weighting in entrance scholarships either. No 'modern' headmaster, still less (the alternative scheme) a separate modern school, ever materialized. Somehow, he got away with it.

He got away with it largely because, whether or not they approved of what he was doing, everybody had to admit that he did it magnificently. Walker believed in academic success, and he governed St Paul's at a time when competitive examinations had ousted proprietary patronage in opening a wide range of important doors. In the league tables of schools' examination successes, regularly published in the newspapers, St Paul's under Walker was easily first. Between 1886 and 1895 Paulines won 173 entrance awards at Oxford and Cambridge, twenty-six more than any other school. There is no doubt that Walker piqued himself on this preeminence, and that he devolved much energy and crafty skill to achieving it. His enemies thought nothing else interested him. The most glittering prizes were classical scholarships at Trinity College, Cambridge, or Balliol. In 1898 the fifteen-year-old Compton Mackenzie was sent for by the High Master for contemptuous treatment of a mathematical examination. He made his excuses. 'Never mind,' said Walker, quite pleasantly, 'you will get a Balliol scholarship in 1901.' But when Mackenzie dared insist that he wanted to go to Magdalen, as a Commoner, to read history, Walker's angry, searing and elegant response concluded: 'You could have been as great a Greek scholar as Jebb or Porson, and you have flung it all away to swagger up and down the corridors of this school with the manners and appearance of a deboshed clerk.' Another able boy, of thirteen, wanted to go on to the science side. Walker's advice to him was: 'My boy, you are making a great mistake. If you go in for science, your future is quite uncertain. If you stick to

*Above left : The High Master's house was later converted into School House, for boarders.*

*Above : The dais with the masters' table can be made out under the window at the far end of the dining-hall. The smaller boys are wearing Eton collars.*

*Below left : The Board Room, unlike the form rooms, looked on to the playing fields. The High Master's chair is in the foreground. Three representations of Colet gaze towards it ; the portrait on the easel is a curious eighteenth-century version of the Dean, with side-whiskers. It now hangs in the fifth School's Montgomery Room.*

*Below : The 'large Chemistry Laboratory'.*

your classics properly, I will undertake to say that you will pay for your education in scholarships and be able to earn £400 a year within a reasonable time afterwards.'

The story looks a perfect piece of evidence for that thesis about the public schools' guilty role in British industrial decline. It is told by an encomiast of Walker, V. M. Coutts-Trotter, who, himself the son of an iron-merchant, won the Balliol Scholarship and a first in Greats, and who became Chief Justice of Madras. He tells the story to point up not Walker's narrow or fanatical commitment to classics, but his common sense and care for individuals. The boy's father was poor; the advice was correct and correctly slanted, for the boy, though brilliant, was not interested in learning but in making a living. Within his lights, Walker's words were enlightened. But another of his sayings was: 'A boy will not take kindly to commerce when he has once tasted Greek iambics'; he was always his own careers master.

Leonard Woolf thought Walker 'seemed to be interested only in the clever boys'. Coutts-Trotter thought he made it his business to know about all the boys in the School, 'what any boy had done, what he was doing, what he was likely to do'. Ernest Shepard sketched him sailing 'majestically down the corridor ... it was useless for any boy doing penance outside a door to try and hide behind the lockers'. Later, he took an interest in Shepard's plans to be an artist, or at least in his prospects for a scholarship to the Royal Academy Schools. He recognized G. K. Chesterton, too, as someone out of the ordinary, and gave him the privileges of an eighth-former, even though he did little school work, filling his exercise books with drawings and dreams. To Ernest Raymond, Walker was a 'scholarly but alarming old gentleman', as frightening to the masters as to the boys, but Chesterton remembers his laughter, 'unearthly convulsions of his own extraordinary laughter which, like the other movements of his extraordinary voice began like an organ and ended like a penny whistle'. E. C. Bentley, at whose jokes Walker did laugh, thought his jollity was like being slapped on the back by the Matterhorn.

One of Walker's admirers dismisses the accusation that he cultivated hot-house plants which withered early as 'the futile babbling of a bevy of Cassandras' and proudly lists a number of names, dazzling, perhaps, in 1932, but all (except Compton Mackenzie) now more or less forgotten. Perhaps there is something in the charge. Raymond Asquith, discussing the prospects of a Balliol Scholarship in 1895, complained: 'I hear there are a particularly strong lot of Paulines up: they are fatal people, turn out reams of machine-made verses at the shortest possible notice, and generally know everything.' But, he concedes, 'I believe that they get quite a good education'.

Of the poets at St Paul's in Walker's day, Laurence Binyon won the right prizes and scholarships, at school and at Oxford, and wrote movingly of Colet in celebration of the School's quatercentenary:

> ... He knew
> No rule of crabbed lore; rather a clue
> Gave, that should make us of our historied kind
> Comrades, and keep in us a morning mind,
> Since to the wise Learning is always new.

*High Master Walker from E. H. Shepard's* Drawn From Life *(1961).*

Yet Binyon is not now much read beyond his lines 'for the Fallen', and Edward Thomas, who is, remembered his brief days at St Paul's unhappily. There is no evidence that Walker saw anything in him. 'I should have done anything he told me, but he never told me to do anything except, "Speak up. I'm an old man".' Thomas thought the boys were grimly earnest and only interested in work and success. His form-master, R. F. Cholmeley, recognized his ability and tried to help him, but was not much appreciated. 'Later,' Thomas recalled, 'I developed some sort of pride in the great names connected with the school': it is a pride oddly expressed in his life of Marlborough, in which he writes of Marlborough and Jeffreys: 'the school, I think, boasts of them both, though it did not make the one a sanguinary judge or the other a comparatively humane general.'

Walker once spoke, or rather roared, at the thirteen-year-old Paul Nash, who was gazing at the huge mosaics in Hall 'of the more famous Old Paulines, from Milton to Marlborough', in 'a voice so huge in volume that for a moment it seemed to me to be identified with the great Duke . . . "You're doing no good here", he boomed.' But Nash's memory was at fault: there was no mosaic of Marlborough – only of St Paul, Colet, Erasmus, Milton and Campden, with the 153 fishes, and above them all, the boy Jesus in the Temple. They were Walker's idea, the work of T. R. Spence, and completed only a few months before Nash came to the School.

Walker did see a good deal in Chesterton ('six foot of genius. Cherish him, Mrs Chesterton, cherish him'). Great man as Chesterton undoubtedly was, it is

Above left: *Some sketches drawn by G. K. Chesterton while he was at St Paul's.*

Above: *'A Corner of the Art Room', from a volume of photographs of the School published about 1910.*

The Special in the Great Hall, where in the 1890s they spent their time 'doing nothing all day long but Greek and Latin Arnold', under the 'patient, lovable' Mr Pantin. This photograph, however, dates from about 1930. The master is H. W. Flewett.

not quite clear that he wholly fulfilled his genius. Compton Mackenzie and Ernest Raymond wrote their most successful novels very early – and both are full of their schooldays. In *Sinister Street*, Walker appears as Dr Brownjohn of St James's. Raymond's main treatment of St Paul's came much later in *Mr. Olim* (1961), in which Walker is Dr Hodder of St Erkenwald's, though the dust-jacket is a pleasant watercolour of Waterhouse's north front. Here the hero recalls his first day at the School:

> Even as I write, fifty and more years later, our fear of the Old Man comes close to me and I half wonder that I dare to make this fun of him; that I dare even now to take his name in vain. Dr. Hodder, over seventy on that morning, was probably the last of those nineteenth-century headmasters who held it their business to be formidable to the point of terror. He was the last of the school of Dr. Keate of Eton, and in his day, which was my day, probably the most famous headmaster in England.

Yet Walker was not a great beater: he seldom punished, because unlike Keate he kept excellent discipline easily. He did, however, preside at 'Porterings', rare but terrifying ceremonial beatings by the Head Porter, a former sergeant in the Brigade of Guards. But he was as ineradicable an experience as Keate, the great flogger, had been to Etonians, perhaps too large and demanding an experience too early in life to be altogether good for some of the most responsive. There are other points in common with Keate too. Though a Rugbeian, Walker had no time for religious intensity, and little interest in athleticism; far from governing through prefects, he got rid of the existing system of employing the eighth form as monitors *en bloc* – retaining, however, and relying on, the Captain of the School, who was always the boy at the top of the Classical Eighth. His interests were really those of an *early* nineteenth-century headmaster, those (in fact) of Sleath. Keate had had to subdue a violent, arrogant and increasingly aristocratic school; Walker put down with verbal ferocity what he detested most, any form of snobbery or cant. He hated moralizing as much as dandyism and smartness. He could seem ogrish.

His method of approach [wrote Mackenzie] was appalling to the young, for he would swing along up the aisle and suddenly plunge into a seat beside the chosen boy, pushing him inward along the form with his black bulk. He would seize the boy's pen and after scratching his own Head with the end of the holder he would follow word by word the conditional sentences, tapping the paper between the lines as he read each sentence, so that at the end of his examination the page was peppered with dots of ink. The Old Man, although he had a voice like ten bulls, was himself deaf and after bellowing in a paralyzing bass he would always finish a remark with an intoned 'um?' of tenor interrogation to exact an answer from his terrified pupil.

*'In all London could there have been a more sudden change than this: out of the ringing and banging of the Hammersmith Road into this green garden within the gates? One seemed to step out of the roar of modernity into the quiet of a Gothic past.' (Ernest Raymond, Mr. Olim, 1961.)*

Not everybody agreed that Walker bellowed. Leonard Woolf remembered
'growls and grumblings and occasionally a roar of rage'. Woolf's account of
Walker and of the School which Walker was remoulding is unusual in its essential
hostility. Walker is 'almost a stage schoolmaster', eccentric to a grotesque degree.
A real love of scholarship has been warped by his passion for turning out scholarship
winners. His only other interests are probably 'good food, good drink, and good
cigars'.

This last Woolf admits is a mere guess. Much more serious is his charge against
the High Master personally and the School as a whole of barbarity, fanaticism
and philistinism. He admits the efficiency of the system; it made good classical
scholars. But so it should: both in the Special and in the Classical Eighth there
was still nothing else but Latin and Greek; and Woolf, a competent mathematician
taught by a good mathematics master (Pendlebury), was not allowed to develop
his mathematical activities. 'Classical fanaticism' ruled. But so, apparently, did barbarity and philistinism. The real ruler was not the classics but athleticism. Interest
in intellectual life was despised, and this not only by the boys, but 'by nearly all
the masters. . . . Every master who taught me until I reached the age of sixteen
or seventeen accepted and inculcated the same doctrine and ethic.'

It is hard to evaluate this last claim of Woolf's. He was good at games himself,
he tells us; it is not the seven-stone weakling's revenge. He is used as evidence
by Jonathan Gathorne-Hardy, in his popular work, *The Public School Phenomenon*

*Below: The School gymnasium.*

*Below right: In 1911 a Pauline
was able to boast that 'the swimming
team has never yet been beaten by a
School, and has on more than one
occasion defeated Oxford
University'.*

(1977), in which St Paul's appears indistinguishable from other schools where 'the advent of the games obsession meant that esteem for academic and intellectual endeavour was, except for a tiny minority, almost entirely obliterated'. Yet there were no compulsory games until 1897 (three years after Woolf came to St Paul's) and even then the requirement was only one afternoon a week. J. W. Marcy, a keen athlete, who was at St Paul's from 1886 to 1892, remembers how 'little side' rugger was played 'under the somewhat casual direction of a member of the First XV who regarded his job of referee as an infernal nuisance'. At the end of Marcy's very first game, a year after he joined the School,

> the first XV boy called me over and said: 'Kid, you seem to know something about this game. You take charge of "little side", in future and see that you get two fifteens out every Tuesday.'

It is, of course, possible that, though informal and officially voluntary, games may still have dominated the School, even if another boy, Edward Thomas, was never asked to play any.

Marcy did not have any difficulty in recruiting his two fifteens. Yet the early issues of *The Pauline* (which began in 1882) are full of exhortation to athletic enthusiasm and complaints of lack of it. G. K. Chesterton (at St Paul's from 1887 to 1892) took no interest in games, never played any games and suffered not at all for not doing so. He did have to go, or rather fail to go, through the hoops in the gymnasium, where his efforts were regarded by other boys and perhaps by

*Rowing IV and cox with R. F. Cholmeley in 1891. Uniforms were a sign of athletic distinction several years before they were imposed on the whole School.*

himself as comical. As for Walker, though he thought 'regular and systematic gymnastics ... an absolute necessity', he took no official notice of Sports Day, even (if Marcy is to be trusted) in 1894 when the Duchess of Albany presented the prizes. It may have been that year too that he made his first reference to games at Apposition. He congratulated the First XI on its success, but 'began with the words, delivered in tones of thunder, "I know nothing about cricket"'.

Marcy does, however, partly agree with Woolf's gravest charge. Woolf writes of 'the contempt of our teachers for what they were teaching'; Marcy that 'most of the masters seemed as little interested in their work as we were, and if we watched the clock they watched the clock and their watches, too'. They mean the men who taught them in their junior years, and Woolf's charges are specific only against the headmaster of his preparatory school. Both of them admired, even loved, A. M. Cook (later Surmaster), and Marcy also writes affectionately of Digby la Motte, aesthete and friend of Oscar Wilde, who was then a new master of twenty-five, and who shared his interest in cleanliness and clothes.

'Marcy, it is such a pleasure to have you in the Form, your collar is always so clean. Do tell me the name of your laundry.' After I had left his Form he met me in the corridor and stopped me, whispering in a kind of confidential manner: 'Marcy, I am so unhappy. My form is no longer what it was. Nobody washes now. Can't you arrange to come back to me?'

No wonder that the foppish master and the fastidious boy both equally disliked the most famous of all Walker's staff, the Reverend Horace Dixon Elam. Elam was not notably clean, appeared to despise and detest school-teaching, and not only looked at his watch but went to sleep in his own lessons and loudly sighed for escape. 'Do you know where I live, boys? I live in a hovel in Shepherd's Bush – Shepherd's Bush, mark you! – and there I save my pence during term-time so as to be able to get as far as possible from you all in the holidays.' This is Raymond's Olim: but there is no lack of evidence that, except for a little characteristic sentimentalizing, Raymond's Olim and the real Elam are one. Elam rather enjoyed his portrayal in *Sinister Street* as Mr Neech, but had died before *Mr. Olim* was written.

Elam also appeared to despise and detest the High Master, and was believed to keep in his desk a bottle of medicine 'to be taken before and after interviewing the Man from Manchester'. He called Gardiner a 'fierce and desperate man' and La Motte 'the decorative gentleman next door'. He would cane a whole class to put them 'in form for a good morning's work', or just out of his own black melancholy. He was undoubtedly mad, Raymond thought, and he used to ask boys if they thought him mad. 'If the boy said "no" he would give him a hundred lines for telling a lie; if "yes" a hundred lines for cheek. The correct answer was, "Not mad, sir, only a little eccentric".'

A few years after Elam's death, Ernest Raymond gave a lecture about him at a vacation course in London. It led to extensive correspondence in several newspapers, and to leading articles in *The Times* and the *Morning Post*. Not all his pupils admired him even in retrospect; one thought him unfit to black Walker's boots.

*The Reverend Horace Dixon Elam 'taught his class little from the school curriculum, but much of life', and provided 'pungent comments on "the miseries of marriage", the "animal nature of boys", the absurdity of the crowd and its conventions'. (B. H. Liddell Hart, Memoirs, 1965.)*

This is how Neech/Elam welcomes a new member of his class:

Twenty-six miserable boys are already having a detestable and stultifying education in this wretched class, and now comes a twenty-seventh. Very well. Very well. I'll stuff him with the abominable jargon and filthy humbug. I'll cram him with the undigested balderdash. Oh, you unhappy boy. You unfortunate imp and atom. Sit down, if you can find a desk. Sit down and drench your mind with the ditchwater I'm paid to teach you.

Olim/Elam's bitterness is rooted in his vision of what Colet had meant St Paul's to be, and his revulsion from what it actually was.

'What he wanted for them was ... grace and goodness for body and mind. As it is ... as it is' – he turned from the window and leaned against the hot-water pipes, resting his thin, wrinkled hands upon them – 'what have we got here? I fancy I've told you once or twice before. Except for a few overstuffed scholars, a Reservation for barbarians with a lopsided worship of sport. They sneer at cleverness with dilated nostrils ... like so many gaping rabbits. May the Dean sleep in peace and not know.'

Yet Walker was not a Gradgrind, even if unduly influenced by Bentham and the new German gymnasia, but a humane, intelligent, cultivated and charitable man, who, though he did bow in the house of the bitch-goddess Success, was himself not only to one Pauline 'the dear "Old Man" whom in boyhood I worshipped, whom in manhood I reverenced and whose image I shall carry with me to the grave'. One day Walker came up with a boy in Elam's class in the Hammersmith Road. He took the boy by the ear, as he often did.

'Whose form are you in?' 'Elam's, sir.' Some kindly questioning followed, and before long I found myself reciting the tale of my grievances. Walker seemed quite moved, and for a time said nothing. At last, 'I know, my boy, I know. But you must put up with it.' A pause, and then, reflectively and almost to himself, 'Elam is the best teacher I've got in the school.'

A necessary remark: possibly a true one, and undated.

Cholmeley and Thomas Rice Holmes arrived in 1886, two years after Elam. These two men alone, Chesterton claimed, got past his guard of pretended indifference to things of the mind. E. C. Bentley thought Cholmeley the best master he came across by far; but he admired Rice Holmes, who was an authority both on Julius Caesar and on the Indian Mutiny. Walker's staff also included Marchant, editor of Thucydides, for whom boys fought fiercely to compose Greek iambics and for whom Lupton composed his only joke, and Botting, to Gollancz 'pretty nearly my ideal of a man', whose successes and frustrations as coach and writer of textbooks paid for the expensive education of Antonia White, which germinated *Frost in May* (1933). The real reason for schooling, in Chesterton's half-serious schoolboy view, was to study the characters of the masters. 'And the masters at St Paul's were very interesting.'

*T. Rice Holmes, about 1896. At the time of his death in 1933 an Old Pauline recalled in the* Evening News *that one of his favourite remarks was 'I do not in the least mind your doing your work badly, but I object to your not doing it at all', and that boys used to 'recite their Latin composition in high and piercing tones to annoy him'.*

# VIII

## 'IF YOU WANT TO WORK, THERE IS NO BETTER SCHOOL'

*B. L. Montgomery*

## 1905–1962

*In the 1930s cigarette cards were avidly collected, especially by schoolboys. This is from the 'Well-known ties' series, 1934.*

WALKER NEVER VISITED ST PAUL'S after his retirement; he was *aut Caesar aut nihil*. But since his day, St Paul's has never lost his stamp. Fifty years on, Raymond, in his fictional persona, sees himself dreaming in a distant garden of that 'truly awful figure, a Presence with a ragged grey beard and a black silk gown hanging about his thick figure like the folded wings of Apollyon and a voice like the opening thunders of Jove'. Even eighty years on, even in Barnes, even in Thatcher's Britain, the presence walks.

But to keep one's feet, as Walker would have required, on the ground: in almost every essential, St Paul's as Walker left it is the St Paul's of today. The hugely increased numbers of masters and boys, the diversified curriculum with the eight forms surviving only as a shadow, boarding houses, the preparatory school and entry delayed until twelve or thirteen, organized compulsory games and the clubs, the School open to all religions, the hungry cult of success – despite our late twentieth-century belief in the unrivalled speed of change in our own day, despite the physical obliteration of Walker's Hammersmith habitat, St Paul's as Walker left it has far more in common with St Paul's now than with St Paul's in 1876. Not all the changes were of Walker's making, and those changes that assimilated St Paul's most closely to other 'great public schools' were probably those that interested Walker least. Among these were the growth of an old boys' club, a cadet force and a viable school magazine.

The Old Pauline Club goes back a few years before Walker, to 1872, though in 1882 it still only had 160 members. In a sense it goes back much further, for it grew out of one of the periodic revivals of the Feast, or annual Old Boys' Dinner and Sermon. This tradition had continued intermittently since Pepys's time, the dinners proving better at survival than the sermons. But, after a celebration, at Freemasons' Hall in 1810, of the tercentenary, even the dinner lapsed. By the 1860s the only occasion on which Old Paulines regularly met was a summer 'breakfast' at Richmond for eighth-formers and old boys, which was held at three in the afternoon, an inconvenient time for most people. In 1864 a group of Old Paulines therefore revived the Feast, or at least organized biennial dinners, in the summer, which lasted until 1883. The Old Pauline Club itself grew partly out of a Football Club, partly out of the desire for a cheaper dinner; but it entered, in its infancy, with great gusto into the battle against the Charity Commissioners. By 1904 the Club had a thousand members. It presented the School with a Boer War Memorial (a drinking fountain enclosed in columns under a dome); it presented *Comus* in the King's Theatre, Hammersmith, to mark the quatercentenary; it had, for a time, as its secretary, Walker's son, Assistant Master (1900–5) and Mayor of Hammersmith, who taught Homer and Virgil without using a book, but resigned from the staff after applying unsuccessfully to succeed his father in the High Mastership.

In the late nineteenth century school cadet corps were springing up in large

*Field Marshal Lord Roberts unveils the South African War Memorial (1906). It came to Barnes, but was damaged by vandals and bought by an Old Pauline who has preserved it in his garden.*

numbers. Founded in 1890, that at St Paul's was not one of the earliest, but was surely unique if the master who founded it, Captain Bicknell, really allowed the boy-officers to be elected by the whole School. As the annual Public School Camps began that same year, St Paul's was able to take part in them almost from the first, as well as in the shooting competitions at Bisley, where trophies were won in 1906 and 1908. From 1906 shooting was compulsory for all boys. Essential to the Corps's success was its relationship with games. It must not poach on them, and therefore concentrated on the Spring Term when, for a few years, and again by popular vote, the game played was the not-very-serious lacrosse, and on Saturday mornings, when uniformed Paulines manœuvred over Barnes and Wimbledon Commons. Thus it was possible, Bicknell remarked, for 'many of the best athletes' to join the Corps, and become 'the best non-commissioned officers'. Numbers fell after the initial enthusiasm, but rose again during the Boer War. Whether or not the school authorities were jingoistic, many of the boys were, coming to school 'with buttons stuck in their coats on which the face of Sir Redvers Buller looked fiercely forth'. One even wore a union-jack waistcoat, and defeated a young master who told him to take it off: 'Oh, sir; we never thought that you were a pro-Boer.'

For in 1899 one controversial facet of modern school life was still unknown: school uniform. The Corps had its uniform, of course, at first a dark grey Norfolk jacket and forage-cap, then 'regulation drab-serge', paid for by the cadets themselves; but otherwise boys wore more or less what they wished or convention

*Field Day in Richmond Park, 1915.*

dictated. A century before, the usual dress was a short jacket and knee-breeches, and the Captain of the School affected top-boots. In the 1860s, when an eighth-former put on a stick-up collar or a tail-coat for the first time, he was fined half-a-crown, which went towards the Richmond breakfast. Raymond began at St Paul's in 1901, but a new boy in his novel still wears nothing uniform except his cap; he wears knickerbockers and a Norfolk jacket, his boots are despised by a friend in 'the long trousers of an Eton suit'. A senior boy wears his First XV cap – black and silver with a long white tassel – even in an electric tram. Such a cap, Montgomery's cap, is preserved in the School Archives. Top hats were the privilege of the eighth form, and scholars of Oxford or Cambridge colleges, who often stayed at school a good year after winning their scholarships, wore their college gowns.

The first school magazine, *The Pauline*, appeared in November 1831, achieved three issues, and collapsed in less than a year. Its contents were literary, historical and even political; it had no parochial interests: the idea of a school magazine that wrote about the School was not yet conceived. There were several other ephemeral journals in the 1830s. The *Pauline Magazine* appeared in November 1836. Its style was distinctly purple, and it did contain a heavily satirical account of a boy's first day at school. Though boy and school were labelled fictional, the magazine, which was the work of the eighth form, was suppressed. The next *Pauline* began in 1882, with official backing, and survives. Its first editorial proclaimed that it would try to bring harmony between those usually feuding sections of the School, 'the athletic and industrious', and that it would welcome 'the early efforts of young members of St Paul's', who were urged to 'try, try, try again'. Despite which, according to Chesterton, '*The Pauline* appeared to us schoolboys as utterly cut off from aspiration; we should as soon have thought of writing to the *Times*.' Instead, he and his friends produced a magazine of their own, the *Debater*, the organ of the Junior Debating Club (JDC), which they also founded.

This was junior to the Union Society, a rather dignified body which, dating from 1853, believed itself to be the oldest school debating society in England. The Union Society modelled itself as best it could on the Oxford and Cambridge unions, had a clubroom, with a library and newspapers, and elected its members, all eighth-formers, by ballot. Its early debates were decorous and perhaps rather dull; but in 1859, during the annual anniversary debate, which was held in the Great Schoolroom, a boy called Alfred Finucane McCarthy refused to take off his hat for the national anthem. He was later wounded at Gaeta, fighting for Garibaldi, and died in Australia in 1873. G. D. H. Cole, the future economist, was President of the Union in 1907–8. He complained of its dingy, semi-subterranean clubroom, but thought its great value was as a self-electing democracy. He was also proud that, by the time he left, its political views had swung strongly to the left – at least among the members who expressed any: many never attended a debate, and valued the Union entirely as a club.

The original JDC only lasted for three years and never had more than a dozen members. Chesterton, the presiding genius and the oldest member, was hardly sixteen when it was born. Two of its members were to become presidents of the Oxford and two of the Cambridge unions. Of the two Oxford presidents, Lucian

*C. H. Bicknell, mathematics master and founder of the School Cadet Force.*

*The second cover for* The Pauline, *designed by Robert Harris, was used from 1882 to 1932.*

*G. K. Chesterton designed this menu for a reunion dinner of the Junior Debating Club. Among those who attended, Langdon-Davies became President of the Cambridge, and Oldershaw of the Oxford, Union Societies. R. E. Vernede, one of the Georgian poets, was killed in action in 1917. Salter, later a Cambridge don, wrote a history of St Paul's School 1909–1959.*

Oldershaw, the secretary, also became Secretary of the Old Pauline Club and Chesterton's brother-in-law, and E. C. Bentley, Chesterton's great friend, achieved fame from one detective novel and a new comic verse form. The members took their debates seriously, and their magazine too, which Oldershaw, at fifteen, saw through the press and kept financially afloat. It contained the first of Chesterton's verses to be published: 'I have never read those verses since; there are limits to the degradation and despair which even autobiography demands.' 'I fear', Chesterton also wrote, when reflecting on all this schoolboy effort, 'there is something incurably conscientious and solemn about the nature of Paulines.' But he added that 'this is a fault I have often had to correct in myself', and he also remembered that at meetings of the JDC it was not uncommon for sticky buns to hit him on the face.

A recent biographer of Chesterton thinks that he and his circle were outsiders, that they did not write for *The Pauline* because they despised it, and that they scorned the Union because it involved collaboration with masters. There is little or no evidence for any of these assertions: the Union was for eighth-formers only, and when they reached the eighth, many of the Debaters took leading parts in

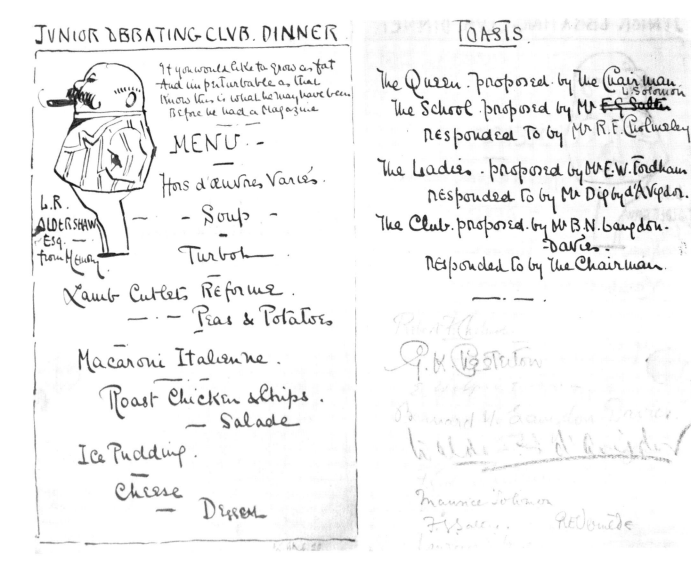

it. The same biographer, in describing the birth of the Clerihew, embellishes Bentley's own account by calling the chemistry lesson in which it was delivered extremely dull, which perhaps it was, and refers to Bentley himself as a 'vibrant young man', which is jargon that he would have found irresistibly comic. But there is good precedent for biographical invention in Clerihew country: among the early ones is this fantastic libel on the Pauline household gods:

> After dinner Erasmus
> Told Colet not to be 'blas'mous',
> Which Colet, with some heat,
> Requested him to repeat.

And Bentley himself wrote an entirely appropriate, and 'strictly untruthful' version of its genesis, in an early spring morning and a schoolboy's study:

I was conning, with the aid of a dictionary, the story of those measures which Julius Caesar had found, to his regret, to be unavoidable in dealing with the Usipetes and the Tencteri. By some association of ideas, the process of which I am unable now to recall, there drifted across my mind – like a rosy sunset cloud softening the white majesty of the Himalaya – the valiant figure of Sir Humphrey Davy. The pen was in my hand. Musing, I hardly knew what it was tracing on the page. Then, with a start, I saw that I had written:

> Sir Humphrey Davy
> Detested gravy.
> He lived in the odium
> Of having discovered sodium.

So it began.

At least two of the members of the JDC were Jewish: the Solomon brothers. Both had distinguished careers, one becoming a professor of Latin, the other a director of GEC. Whatever the truth about Chesterton's anti-Semitism, at St Paul's, as well as later, some of his best friends were Jews. It was, he thought, more than most a school for 'swots', and 'there were a great many swots because there were a great many Jews'. If the language is not now acceptable, the line of Jewish Pauline intellectuals has gone on from Chesterton's day to the present: Leonard Woolf, Victor Gollancz, Max Beloff, Jonathan Miller, Peter Shaffer. It would be hard to identify the first Jewish Pauline – perhaps Samuel Hohneman in 1879; Louis Montagu, 2nd Lord Swaythling, who entered the School in 1883, was one of the earliest, as well as being one of the last boys to begin school on the old site. A new, and religiously easy-going, High Master will have helped, as well as a situation not far from growing areas of Jewish settlement in west and north-west London. Another non-Christian was among the first new boys at Hammersmith. This was Manmohan Ghose, who, as Sri Aurobindo, is now venerated by tens of thousands of his fellow Hindus as a saint and sage.

But, if being a member of the JDC did not make one an outsider at St Paul's a century ago, did being Jewish? Chesterton thought it could; and the very language in which he defends himself against the charge of anti-Semitism convicts him, by today's standards, of at any rate the comparatively mild anti-Semitism of so many Englishmen of his day. 'I was criticized,' he writes, 'for quixotry and prig-gishness in protecting Jews,' and goes on to explain why they needed protecting in language which nobody now would permit himself. But it was not dishonest language; it was not usually Jews, but his own ideas about Jewishness, which Chesterton disliked.

Compton Mackenzie remembered unpleasant treatment of Jewish boys, and regretted taking part in it, but neither Leonard Woolf nor, a few years later, Victor Gollancz needed much protection. Neither was particularly popular; neither, it seems, was at any disadvantage because of being Jewish, except that Gollancz might well otherwise have become Captain of the School and that his orthodox back-ground imposed a long walk on Fridays in winter and forbade him to take part in Saturday games. He and a friend did once walk out of the Union (of which he was the very chaotic Secretary) because of some flippant speaking 'with an anti-Semitic flavour'; but other boys hurried out and persuaded them to return. Another new High Master, clerical, and much more conventional, appears to have made no difference to the now well-established Jewish presence in St Paul's.

Walker was, as the saying goes, a hard act to follow. Perhaps it was inevitable that the successor to this gigantic eccentric should seem conventional and rather colourless. The Reverend A. E. Hillard had, naturally, a first in Mods and a first in Greats. He was ten years a master at Clifton, and six headmaster of Durham School, a small school whose curriculum he broadened. He was already the author of successful textbooks, though the famous 'Hillard and Botting' was yet to come. Hillard's portrait, by the Old Pauline Eric Kennington, unkindly portrays a reserved, humourless, very headmasterly figure, and Magnus Pyke recalls Hillard's only words to him: 'If you don't like the way things are done here at St Paul's, you can leave and go to the Regent Street Polytechnic.' A master could go from September to March without exchanging a word with him. It was not all loss. When Hillard retired, the Surmaster remarked on how pleasant it had been to cease living on top of a volcano. The distinguishing mark of Hillard's reign, he said, had been its fairness. This fairness had, indeed, impelled him to begin his High Mastership by putting right an act of injustice which he thought Walker had committed, just as his sense of duty made him spend obviously uncomfortable hours on the touchline, 'always wearing a top-hat and a clerical frock-coat'.

Hillard was quick to institute a confirmation service at St Paul's Cathedral, Sunday morning services, and occasional communion services in a Hammersmith church. He did not, however, really reverse the laicizing that had begun under his predecessor: the only two masters besides the new High Master who were clergymen were Lupton, the Surmaster, and Elam. In this respect St Paul's was ahead of other schools. At Walker's last Apposition Dinner, the Bishop of London took the opportunity to suggest that the School needed a chapel. None was pro-vided until after the Great War, when the Library was converted into a War Memorial Chapel, dedicated in 1926. The Library itself had moved into the former Chemistry Laboratory, and was decorated with panels from the old School at the City: it was renamed the Walker Library, a name which has stuck unofficially

*Victor Gollancz, from a group of prefects in 1912.*

even in Barnes. It was opened in 1914. The new, and leisurely completed, Chapel was far too small to contain the whole School: daily prayers continued to be held in the Great Hall, all in Latin in Hillard's day, and with a little Latin right up to the departure from Hammersmith.

Elsewhere, Hillard was not slow to innovate. He took science much more seriously than Walker had. New laboratories, more of them than the Senior Science Master had dared ask for, were opened in 1909. In 1920 a boy in the Science Eighth was appointed Captain of the School, the first ever not to be a classicist. He still had to be a Christian, because his duties included reading prayers in Hall. Hillard instituted prefects very soon after his appointment, B. L. Montgomery being one of the first. The future Field–Marshal thought that 'St. Paul's is a very good school for work so long as you want to learn'; under some pressure he himself did work hard enough to get into Sandhurst. He remained a private in the OTC. His reputation at school was as a games player. He was captain of the XI and the XV, and known as 'the Monkey': 'This intelligent animal makes its nest in football fields . . . It is vicious, of unflagging energy, and much feared.'

At his first Apposition Dinner, Hillard referred to the purchase of new playing fields, at Wormwood Scrubs. What had been considered spacious grounds in 1894 were inadequate now that athleticism was beginning to be given its head. At that same dinner, the Bishop of Bristol said that he always asked about sports and that all the scholastic successes of the world could not alone make a real man; he also said that everyone must feel that shooting was a most important thing in public schools now. The Captain of the School said that more important either than scholarship or athletics was 'a thoroughly sound Public School spirit'. It was only a year since Walker had disdained any effort to emulate the 'splendid *esprit de corps*' of the great public schools. 'Our work lies in a far lower sphere', he had insisted, with obvious pride. 'We strive, not without success, to make our boys intellectually strong, industrious, loyal, and, as far as man can do, morally pure and upright.

*A chemistry laboratory in use in the 1930s. In 1937 a scientific society was founded, and Sir Francis Simon FRS came to the School 'with a car-load of apparatus and gave a most entertaining and instructive lecture'.*

*Boxing: 'St Paul's have failed to win only two straight school team matches with their first team in twenty-five years', wrote Hylton Cleaver (*Sporting Rhapsody, *1951), adding that the captain would sometimes be left out of the team, because other schools had no one to match him.*

*Jerry Driscoll, the swimming and boxing coach, photographed for a schoolboy magazine,* The Captain, *around the turn of the century.*

The rest we are forced to leave, and I do not regret it, to fathers and mothers and the influence of home.'

Yet Walker had made a generous personal gift towards building a school swimming-bath in 1900. Swimming and fives (neither of which take up much room) were early among the most successful athletic sports: new fives courts were built in 1912 and new changing-rooms in 1913. Though there was as yet no boat-house, and as late as 1911 a writer complained that 'for some reason the Rowing Club has never received the support which it deserves', there was a Pauline Blue in both boats in 1902 and again in 1903. But boxing provided St Paul's with its most formidable reputation, as P. G. Wodehouse testified in his early novel, *The Pothunters* (1902):

'Any idea who's against us?'
'Harrow, Felsted, Wellington. That's all, I think.'
'St Paul's?'
'No.'
'Good.'

But a few pages later, a Pauline boxer, 'after the custom of Paulines' fights his opponent 'to a standstill in the first round'.

Hillard was not one of those who thought, at the beginning of the Great War, that Germany would be knocked out equally quickly. 'This is likely to be a long war', he told the School in September 1914, 'and to demand great tenacity of purpose to counterbalance the inevitable weariness and loathing, the losses that will touch all, the distress which is bound to accumulate and grow.' The suffering of St Paul's for the next four years was the same as the suffering of other schools, though that was no comfort: to watch helplessly as the list of its killed and wounded lengthened, and as its sons grew and departed and died. The public schools suffered worst, because young officers were the men most likely to be killed, though many Paulines served, and many died, in the ranks, as did Private H. Hind, the cricket professional. Altogether 506 Paulines were killed or died of wounds, one-sixth of those who served, five-sixths of the numbers then in the School at any one time. Two won the Victoria Cross.

Ewart Alan Mackintosh was at St Paul's from 1910 to 1912. He was editor of *The Pauline* and left with a Scholarship to Christ Church, Oxford. He was commissioned in 1914, fighting in France the next summer, decorated for courage, wounded and back in England in 1916. He met a Quaker girl, Sylvia Marsh, got engaged to her, returned to France, and was shot through the head at Cambrai in November 1917. He had begun writing poetry while at school, and went on writing it at the front. Some of it is collected in a small volume which also contains a brief biographical memoir, a photograph as frontispiece, and three short prose passages, one of them dedicated to the memory of a Pauline friend, E. J. Solomon (the boy who had walked out of the Union with Gollancz), killed in April 1917. There are a dozen such volumes in the School Archives, a few other collections of verse, some just little biographies, by a friend or father or sister, some diaries or collections of letters. It is still impossible to pick them up without emotion.

In some of Mackintosh's poems the destruction of a generation and its ideals are articulated, and he turns grimly on his own earlier light-hearted chivalry:

> Oh God of battles I pray you send
> No word of pity – no help, no friend,
> That if my spirit break at the end
> None may be there to see.

Two of the best-known Pauline participants in the war were young army chaplains with as much idealism at stake as most people. They both survived. The Reverend P. T. B. ('Tubby') Clayton was in Flanders for most of the war, and founded there a rest-house and Christian club for troops coming back from the front line, which, as Toc H, went on expanding and flourishing for years after the war. He was indefatigable and irrepressible, and seems to have managed to love everybody – 'Grand Old Sergt. McInnes', 'two nice Subalterns', 'the Bish. is simply splendid'. He had huge missionary success, throve on danger, and emerged stronger in faith and confirmed in eccentricity. Almost his only unkind words were for *The Pauline*, for praising him: 'Who put in that *dreadful* note about me in *The Pauline*? . . . Please strafe the unknown author, and let my doings remain in obscurity.'

In July 1916 Ernest Raymond, ordained in 1914, went by troop-ship to Gallipoli. His novel *Tell England*, which was published in 1922 after being rejected by seven publishers and at once became a bestseller, tells the story of that campaign as experienced by three friends whose schooldays form the first half of the book. Though named 'Kensingstowe', their school, 'the finest school in England', is a conventional boarding public school, with little or no resemblance to St Paul's. By the time *Tell England* was published, Raymond had resigned his Orders: yet he never lost his idealism, or, some would say, his youthful naïvety; there is no overt sign that the horrors of war destroyed his religious confidence, and in old age he returned to the Christian Church.

*Tell England* is the subject of a perceptive chapter in Jeffrey Richards's recent work on the public schools in English fiction, *Happiest Days* (1988). Richards argued that the widespread belief that the First World War destroyed the ascendency of the public schools and their ideals is mistaken. The rejecting publishers thought that people did not want to read about the war, and especially did not want to read the sentiments about the war to be found in *Tell England*. For there, on a site sanctified by Homer's associations, Raymond's young men live, and some of them die, still upholding the ideals they had learned to love at school. The success of *Tell England*, Richards believes, is one pointer to the survival, long after the First World War, of the public school spirit of which it attempts a near apotheosis. The still greater success, between the wars, of Buchan, Sapper, and indeed Billy Bunter of Greyfriars, tells the same story; and Richards can show from the letters collected by Laurence Housman, *War Letters of Fallen Englishmen* (1930), that the ideals of Rupert Brooke did not all perish in Flanders mud.

Among the young writers were the Paulines Denis Oliver Barnett and John Sherwin Engall. Both were killed. 'I have a strong feeling that I shall come through safely,' wrote Engall, three days before he fell, but 'I am quite prepared to go, and . . . I could not wish for a finer death; and you, dear Mother and Dad, will know that I died doing my duty to my God, my Country and my King.'

*Tell England* is a very innocent book. Half a century later Raymond wrote of his amazement on re-reading it at the 'indubitable but wholly unconscious homosexuality in it'. Another Pauline who survived the war (and won an MC and bar) was H. W. Yoxall, later head of the London office of *Vogue*. In all his seven years at St Paul's, Yoxall recalled, 'I never experienced any homosexual approaches or knew for certain of the existence of these practices'. Marcy had been indignant at a crude hint when he helped a younger boy at his cricket, and so had Compton Mackenzie (who rather provoked it by his choice of friends) at an accusation from Cholmeley: but in what was still essentially a London day school, homosexual intrigue never loomed very large in the life of St Paul's or the worries of its authorities, though in the 1920s Arthur Calder-Marshall kept falling in and out of love with other boys. 'Certain other schools,' Yoxall goes on, 'particularly if they were beating us at games, were said to be sinks of undefined iniquity.'

Yoxall was Captain of the School in 1914. He found it hard to stay on to take the Balliol Scholarship before joining up.

> The Officers' Training Corps was a partial salve to conscience, and the cadet uniform at least a protection against white feathers. It was difficult to lead a school affected by impermanence, with the elder boys slipping away each week into the HAC or the Public Schools' battalion of the Royal Fusiliers.

Seven boys of the 1913 Second XV survived. But the ordinary life of the School went on with little disruption through the four grim years. There were air-raids, and afternoon school was shortened so that boys could go home before they began. There were elderly and temporary masters, to replace those in the Army. The return of A. M. Cook was much welcomed; not all were so successful. The OTC flourished: as well as going on regular route marches it drilled once a week in the lunch hour and learned to stick bayonets in sacks. Hillard worked as Bursar as well as High Master, and suffered from the lengthening Roll of Honour 'to an extent which his reserve did not allow strangers to guess'.

Despite these strains and sorrows, Hillard's High Mastership, which continued until 1927, was an era of confidence and stability, of so much stability that the change, in 1920, to the new pronunciation of Latin, appeared to one historian of the School a matter of major consequence. Academic success was still the first goal, and was achieved, perhaps as successfully as in Walker's day; the curriculum was modestly broadened. Unobtrusively, almost invisibly, Hillard, who did not make sudden appearances in his Assistants' form rooms, and was a good host at dinner, 'but you probably got asked only once', maintained standards and traditions that were questioned by few and them not very influential. One of his senior masters said: 'I can't remember anyone ever saying that Hillard let the School down in any way', a sadly negative, but far from worthless, testimonial.

Hillard was the last of the long stayers. When he retired there had been seven High Masters in nearly two hundred years. The next sixty were to see seven more. His successors, and perhaps especially his first two successors, John Bell (1927–39) and Walter Oakeshott (1939–46), were High Masters with a new style, less grand, more approachable; the change quickly affected the Common Room too, as the legendary figures from the days of the great panjandrum gradually faded away. But it would be a mistake to exaggerate the pace of change, part of which was still, in any case, more convergence with other public schools than response to criticism of the public school way itself. The importance of games continued to grow, as did that of two organizations, both supportive of traditional values, which appeared and quickly flourished: the Scouts and the Christian Union.

Early in this century, the athletic reputation of St Paul's was mainly based on games which most schools regarded as second rank – boxing, swimming and fives. However, by 1908 boys were required, in the Autumn Term, 'in the absence of good and sufficient reason', to play (rugby) football or row. In 1926 the grounds for football and cricket at Wormwood Scrubs were exchanged for better ones at Ealing, and in 1929, surprisingly late for a school so close to the Thames, a boat-house was acquired on the Upper Mall. The clubs, into which the School was divided for games, go back to the end of Walker's day; but Hillard's policy of appointing masters with athletic prowess and enthusiasm gave them leadership and growing *esprit de corps*. They were called A, B, C, D and E: repeated efforts to give them glamorously historic names like Milton and Marlborough repeatedly failed. In 1938 F and G were added, because of the expansion of the School to over eight hundred boys. H Club was at first for boarders, and very successful as a result.

The School Scout troop was founded in 1928, and the Old Pauline troop in

1929, in which year the Chief Scout, himself a Mercer, paid a visit. The movement's peak had probably been reached by the time of the retirement of the Reverend A. C. Heath, its major inspirer, in 1956. There were 122 Scouts in 1957, about one-fifth of the School. The Christian Union began earlier and has flourished longer; it grew out of meetings outside the School for devout Paulines and other boys and an evangelical get-together, 'the Pi-Squash', inside it. About 1922 the Pauline groups rebelled against the fundamentalist organizers outside, and gained semi-official recognition from Hillard in the course of doing so; he also gave them a motto: *Pia et humilis inquisitio veritatis* ('A devout and humble search for truth').

The Christian Union remains the most strongly supported society in the School. It has always had enemies, of all ages. Its historian and Grand Old Man, Eric Hayward, recalls senior masters getting Hillard to block a visit by Gilbert Murray ('little better than a Bolshevik'); more recently its committee has been called a self-perpetuating mafia, coinciding too closely with the prefects. Its influence has touched Paulines of all sorts: Calder-Marshall mocks it and his own susceptibility – to him its atmosphere was a steamy mixture of religious and sexual calf-love. But both Yoxall and, much later, John Thorn, later headmaster of Winchester, took to the 'hearty talks' and the 'groups of casually dressed boys and young men vowing friendship with Christ and one another'. Neither was satisfied for long:

*A first XV match in progress on a Saturday afternoon about 1950.*

others were; the Christian Union fostered the vocation of many, among them W. L. Anderson, Bishop of Salisbury, and C. J. Patterson, Archbishop of West Africa. Its summer house-party is still the great event of the year for many boys.

Hillard had once said to a visiting oriental prelate that the principal aim of education was the glory of God. John Bell, that 'genial and jovial Oxford don', was a layman, as were all his successors until 1986. Bell, wrote one master, removed a sense of strain from the atmosphere; but when he himself became a headmaster he found that 'all which stood me in good stead I had learnt from Hillard'. Bell, however, struggled harder and more successfully for his staff than Hillard over salaries: it may have been poverty that impelled so many masters of the period – Botting, Pendlebury (*Arithmetic*), Hartog (*Brush up your French*) – to write successful textbooks, and others, a long-lasting common-room tradition, to compose crossword puzzles for the newspapers. Bell managed to make the Governors realize that inadequacy of pay was losing St Paul's good young masters, and to abolish the practice, which Hillard had mildly protested about, of making those who were ill pay for temporary substitutes. He got an allowance for the Senior English master, instituted Russian classes and a Director of Music, and entered boys for the School Certificate, which St Paul's had previously disdained. But Bell's most important, and beneficial, achievement was the allocation to every boy of a master as his Tutor. This tutorial system, which, when it works well, gives a boy and his family a close friend, ally and mediator on the staff, has become central to the life of modern St Paul's.

Bell's departure in 1938 for the headmastership of Cheltenham, which would nowadays seem a sideways move at best, may be an index of the continued prestige of boarding schools. Boarding at St Paul's was revived in 1890, in two houses near the School, Colet House, previously the home of the preparatory school, and the High House, whose first Housemaster, for nearly twenty years, was Cholmeley, 'the unique, beloved Cholmondeley', as Paul Nash spells him, in almost his only kind words about the School. By the end of Bell's High Mastership the School was so full that the Governors felt no need to interest themselves in a suggestion from the Headmasters' Conference that public schools should get together to discuss declining numbers. But the number of boarders had not increased correspondingly, and in July 1939 the Governors were considering abolishing one of the houses. There would be little demand for boarding places in London in a modern war.

The Munich crisis erupted almost immediately after Bell's departure. Maurice Tyson, the Surmaster, was Acting High Master until the end of the year. Tyson was said to have been told by his predecessor, when he asked about the Surmaster's duties: 'Well, there isn't much, you know. If he's ill you must go and stand on the platform', adding that one master needed to be sacked. Now Tyson found himself, almost unaided, deciding whether St Paul's could carry on in wartime London at the same time as making the ordinary preparations for the new school year. The only alternative seemed a closure which might be for ever. Tyson decided to carry on unless ordered otherwise by the government: he felt strengthened by the imperturbability of the Chief Clerk, Mr Priest, who sat in his tiny office calmly ruling lines in ledgers 'oblivious or contemptuous of such vulgar interruptions to honourable routine as upstarts like Hitler seemed to be causing'. But on 26 September, three days before the Munich agreement, he was ready to announce that if a state of emergency was declared, the School would close, perhaps indefinitely.

Between the Munich crisis and the outbreak of war a year later, Governors' meetings were much concerned with a battle of their own with Hammersmith Borough Council. During the first crisis, the Council had dug trenches, intended to be air-raid shelters for about fifteen hundred people, across a third of the School playing-fields. After the crisis it would not fill them in again or reply to enquiries about them. The Council claimed, falsely, that it had Home Office authority for digging on private land. Fortunately, the Governors' influence was strong enough for a peremptory order to the Council from the Home Office, and the trenches were filled in. A few months later the School had departed and air-raid shelters were being built, on the other side of its grounds.

By this time there was a new High Master, Walter Oakeshott. Of twenty-seven applicants for the High Mastership, five of the seven short-listed were established headmasters. Oakeshott was one of the other two, a master at Winchester, to which he returned as headmaster after the war. He had spent a year's leave from Winchester working on an enquiry into unemployment; a move to London, he felt, would bring him nearer to the real world. Still in his thirties, he was a courageous choice, and the right one. A scholar of exceptional sensibilities, he had already discovered the earliest manuscript of the *Morte D'Arthur*, and was later to crown his work with the identification of the artists of the Winchester Bible; one of the Library's two Oxyrhynchus papyri, a fragment of *The Odyssey*, is transcribed and annotated in his clear and beautiful hand. His kindliness and charm made him universally loved: he also turned out to possess the strengths needed to bring the School through perhaps the most demanding crisis of its history. The Governors who chose him were very far-sighted or very lucky.

Their foresight did not, however, extend to planning for the School in wartime. The Chairman, Brigadier H. Clementi Smith, had given Tyson his full backing, but left him to make the decisions. It immediately became clear to Oakeshott that, should war come, the School would have to move at once. It was widely believed that London would suffer immediate and dreadful devastation: in any case the government was planning to requisition the buildings. Within a day or two of Oakeshott's arrival, three months before the Germans entered Prague, he was hurrying up to Mercers' Hall to discuss arrangements for an evacuation. There was not much enthusiasm there. He had to make not only decisions but financial commitments himself, find somewhere to go, and organize a practice exodus, by

*On 6 May 1946 Oakeshott wrote to the Librarian: 'Having a few minutes to spare yesterday afternoon, I went up to the Walker Library to look at your fragments of papyrus: and was delighted to find that the smaller one is from a very fine copy of the Odyssey. . . . The other, being upside down and rather awkwardly placed therefore except for an ostrich or giraffe, I did not get very far with.'*

bicycle, in which two hundred boys took part. He collected money from parents, and bought timber and tinned food. By the time Hitler had completed his deal with the Russians and was ready to attack Poland, Oakeshott had completed his planning and was ready to set out. War came, in a sense, just in time: St Paul's was able to move to its new home in Berkshire and settle in in time for the beginning of the school year.

Many schools were uprooted by the Second World War; for most it was an unhappy and demoralizing experience. This was not the case with St Paul's. Prompted by a helpful Wellington master, Oakeshott and Tyson settled the School in part of a country house four miles from Wellington, Easthampstead Park, to whose owners Oakeshott hinted that, if they rejected St Paul's, worse evacuees might be imposed on them. Wellington loaned its playing fields on two days a week, as well as a gymnasium and recently superseded laboratories. Its amiable and urbane Master, R. B. Longden, an old friend of Oakeshott's, made St Paul's welcome – but was himself killed by a bomb which fell on his Lodge in 1941. Paulines and Wellington boys stayed apart, and enjoyed their prejudices about

*Oakeshott teaching in the Old Library, Easthampstead Park. Note the helmets from an earlier war.*

June 1942: the School Cadet
Force at Easthampstead Park.
Montgomery's interest in the JTC
was so great that he found time to
send it a message from Holland for
the General Inspection in February
1945: 'You will have great
opportunities and the training you
receive in the Corps will help you to
make the most of them.'

each other, which were, one Old Pauline recalls, that Wellington was over-conventional and anti-intellectual and that St Paul's was 'the ragged school'.

Most Paulines, masters and boys, lived in the village of Crowthorne, also four miles from Easthampstead, and used the village church for Sunday services and the village school in the evenings for societies and prep. They bicycled to work and games: Tyson believed that he had bicycled 18,000 miles by the end of the war. Staff and local people worked hard to organize billets in and around the village. Most of these were satisfactory, but some were not: there were problems about hot water, and personal problems too. But relations with the village were generally good, and prefects' tours in the evenings, known inevitably as vice patrols, could soon be given up. Soon some large empty houses were purchased and turned into hostels. By 1943 there were fourteen of these, run, at first at their own financial risk, by masters and their families, but they never replaced billeting altogether.

Numbers, of course, declined. On 1 September, 150 boys arrived at Crowthorne. They and the masters made furniture, dug trenches and rearranged their half of the house as a school. Before the term was over nearly 600 boys had turned up, but they were down to 500 in 1942 and 400 in 1943. The decline was never so bad as to put the School's future in question, and was masked by the arrival of part of Colet Court, which was formally incorporated as the official preparatory school of St Paul's in 1943, and prospered in the country. Oakeshott was convinced that the School ought not to be allowed to return to its pre-war size: 600, he thought, was about right.

Many masters left on active service, among them the great Byzantinist P. D.

The boys bicycle back from lessons to their billets

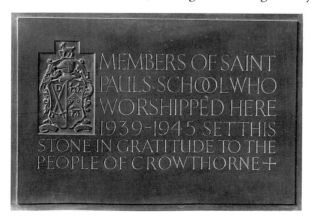

Tablet in Crowthorne Parish
Church, designed by Darcy Braddell
(OP) and presented by Paulines
who were evacuated to
Easthampstead during the war.

Whitting, who won the George Medal for gallantry while fire-fighting in Hammersmith. On the whole, Oakeshott was successful in finding able replacements, among them Leslie Matthews, out of retirement. He quickly reported that the 'psychological effects' of the evacuation were 'altogether favourable', and did not need to revise this view. Though games, except boxing and athletics, suffered, the Home Guard and the School Farm filled the gap, the Field Club tripled its members, and the JTC and the Scouts naturally flourished. There were fire wardens, roof-spotters, a signal platoon and an Air Training Corps. One Scout was honoured for rescuing a pilot from a crashed bomber. In February 1943 Oakeshott was 'granted leave of absence for an indefinite period in connection with his war activities'. He joined a transatlantic convoy, but his destination (or so it was later alleged) was the Pierpont Morgan Library, where he wanted to research into a twelfth-century manuscript. The School carried on unperturbed. John Thorn recalled that there were few rules, hard work and safe bicycling being the important ones. In 1944 a dancing club was formed. The doctor's wife was asked to supply some 'pretty, young and respectable' girls. She found nineteen. In the last summer of the war, Oakeshott produced the *Oresteia* on the terrace at Easthampstead, with Anthony Jay as Cassandra.

Meanwhile, the military were occupying the Hammersmith buildings, and the grounds were shared between the Army, allotments and an RAF barrage balloon. In May 1940 a speedy return to London was considered; Oakeshott was sceptical, however, about hopes that 'our present immunity from air-raids will continue'. The blitz on London began later that summer, and the School buildings were damaged in September and again more seriously in 1944; the Girls' School, which remained in London, was unscathed. The Luftwaffe's attacks were supplemented by the more gradual damage inflicted by the British Army, but this was balanced by glory when the School became the headquarters of 21 Army Group in 1942. Montgomery turned the Board Room (which he had never entered before) into his office, and worked there on his plans for the invasion of Europe. On 15 May

*The School buildings and swimming bath seen from Edith Road during an air raid. The building on fire is probably St Mary's Church, the site of which the School unsuccessfully tried to acquire after the war.*

1944, King George VI and Churchill attended a final briefing of the Allied Commanders at the School.

Absence from London cleared the air for post-war planning. This concerned not only trying to get back home, and restoring and improving the Hammersmith site, but larger questions of the kind of school post-war conditions would demand. By the beginning of 1945 the need to return was urgent; the hostels were increasingly hard to maintain, and two of them belonged to Wellington, which needed them back. It was difficult to regain possession of the School buildings, which were transferred from the Army to the Austrian Control Commission and from that to a Polish organization. Fortunately, the Minister for Economic Warfare, Lord Selborne, was a Mercer and Governor. With his help and Montgomery's and several Old Pauline generals' and MPs', the derequisitioning was achieved on 31 August 1945, and the School reopened at Hammersmith on 1 October, with 384 boys.

Some people had doubted whether it ever would, or should, do so. It was already known before the war that the Talgarth Road was to be broadened, and that a large area of the playing fields would be lost. As the School and its requirements grew, so did the noise and dust of Hammersmith: the old difficulties in the City were beginning to repeat themselves. Rather quietly, in 1938, the Colet Trust acquired 46 acres at Osterley, beyond Ealing on the Piccadilly line. Early in 1942 the Old Pauline headmaster of the Hall School, Hampstead, wrote to the Governors: 'Every young Pauline who comes to see me assures me that the school is never coming back to Hammersmith, but to Osterley Park ... everybody says so.' The Governors published a firm denial in *The Times*: 'No further move is under consideration.'

Privately, the Governors and High Master were thinking over the whole future of the School and not only its location which, they accurately agreed in November 1943, would have to remain Hammersmith 'for at least 20 to 25 years'. Oakeshott was anxious that St Paul's should provide better for 'the ordinary boy (and its

*In July 1946 Field Marshal Montgomery unveiled the plaque commemorating his use of the Board Room in 1944.*

*1945: boys getting the Board Room at Hammersmith ready for the School's return. The map in the centre was used to plan the D-Day landings. It now hangs in the Montgomery Room at Barnes.*

acute form, which may euphemistically be called the *very* ordinary boy)'. He was also enthusiastic about the Fleming Report, which invited public schools to accept a substantial number of elementary school children. The incorporation of Colet Court would make entry at eleven easier, and enthusiasm for such a scheme might reduce the impact of a probable attack on independent education by a future Labour government. Thus, both socially and academically, Oakeshott's vision was of a broader school. He wanted more emphasis on engineering; he invited a Harley Street specialist to give talks about sex.

But the return to damaged buildings and the chill austerity of post-war conditions concentrated attention on less ambitious needs. The buildings had to be made habitable: they were 'covered with a large layer of grit' and 'there were heaps of rubbish in almost every corner'; the swimming-bath, two fives courts and the biology lab were unusable. The housemasters, Alan Cook (and his sister, Nora) and Alec Harbord (and his wife, Joan), spent days scrubbing and cleaning the boarding houses. Oakeshott moved into a flat, and his house, whose condition was little better, was used for boarders. It became a boarding house (School House) permanently a few years later, when Colet House was compulsorily purchased. A large part of the grounds was still covered by allotments, which proved impossible to dislodge until 1950, although some were provocatively growing flowers.

In these uninviting surroundings Oakeshott thought that numbers ought not to rise too fast, and that the ratio of masters to boys should be kept higher than it had been before the war. But the immediate material needs of the School provided obvious counter-arguments for more fee-payers (and increased fees) quickly. When Oakeshott's opportunity to return to Winchester came in 1946, though no one doubted the greatness of his High Mastership, there may have been some relief at Mercers' Hall at the prospect of a more conventional and conservative successor.

R. L. James's obituarist wrote that he was no innovator, and resisted the winds of change with persistence and relish. James said of Oakeshott, who was an enthusiastic student of astronomical history and wanted the School to build a planetarium, that it was difficult to keep him on the ground. Professor F. W. Paish, the economist, a Governor, recalled the good relations between the Governors and James in coping with the 'difficulties of the post-war economy', and that 'unlike many teachers, he had no hobby-horse of his own to ride', except the traditions of the School and the Founder's intentions. As none of the boys who returned in 1945 had known St Paul's before the evacuation, the need to repair bridges with the past was obvious. It was an advantage that James had taught at St Paul's from 1935 to 1939, coaching the classical Upper Eighth and the Second XV, and using a holiday from his Housemastership enforced by mumps to complete a London PhD. His colleagues had liked him, and he got on well with them as High Master. 'Appoint the best and leave them alone', he said and, easy-going in temperament, he generally did so.

James's reign and his successor's are a consolidatory and outwardly rather uneventful period. Gilkes had also been an assistant master at St Paul's, and was also conservative. His remark 'we have no teenage werewolves here' was the first cool intimation of the approach of the age of Aquarius. In most ways, however, he was very unlike his predecessor. Tall and spare, with 'a firm and flinty face' and clear blue eyes, son of a Master of Dulwich, son-in-law of a bishop, he was the very image of a model High Master, and the right host for the Queen, when she visited the School on its 450th anniversary. He cared about the School's reputation and fostered it, firmly tightening discipline and punctuality, about which James had been rather relaxed. But neither with the staff nor with the Governors were his relations so good as James's, the irony being that his worst quarrels with the Governors arose out of his wish to do the best he could for his staff.

Both these High Masters wanted to restore a School whose pre-war standards they admired from direct experience. The quality and appearance of the boys as well as the buildings needed attention. Demand quickly enabled James to return to pre-war selectiveness: he did not just want good exam-passers, but boys who would contribute to games, art, acting and, especially, music. As soon as possible, he put the boys, who in 1945 were mostly in corduroys and lumber-jackets, back into uniform – not the pin-stripes, with bowler hats and umbrellas for seniors which he remembered from the 1930s, but the blazers and grey flannels which were still the rule until 1990.

The buildings' fabric was more troublesome than the boys'. The 700 broken windows, many of them armorial stained glass, if the most startling statistic, were not the most serious problem. Post-war restrictions forbade any hiring of building workers without a permit. But even when refurbished, the building's inadequacies were painfully obvious. 'It was hopelessly out of date', the Governors noted in 1947, and worried about how to satisfy the next ministerial inspection. James dreamed, but could only dream, of adding wings to either side of the north front.

Any plans for a move to Osterley were now dead. Instead, the land there was put to work as playing fields to replace the inadequate grounds at Gunnersbury and supplement the depleted ones at the School. Even for this, official permission had to be obtained. But a move some time, somewhere, was still likely, so that it was sensible to be cautious about ambitious expenditure on the Hammersmith

*The royal visit to the School on 22 May 1959. Like Queen Elizabeth I in 1559, the Queen heard a loyal address in Latin.*

site. In 1950 war-jitters even prompted plans for another evacuation. No London school, said the Ministry of Education, would be allowed to stay where it was. As Easthampstead was not available, Radley and Abingdon were asked to help, and correspondence rumbled on until 1954.

Financial caution was also necessitated by the wartime and post-war misfortunes of the Colet Trust. Its extensive property in Stepney was among the most severely bombed parts of London. Rents naturally collapsed, and the cost of repairs soared. After the war the Labour government imposed rent-control and, eventually, compulsory purchase. This at any rate saved the Colet Trust the embarrassment of financing a public school largely out of the housing of the poor. Though the Trustees had for some years been prudently accumulating a maintenance fund to balance the declining value of the Stepney property, and this fund was now worth £1 million, a financial review drawn up in 1949 was extremely gloomy: were it not for the Maintenance Fund, they thought, St Paul's would be facing bankruptcy. Fees had to be raised by what, in the 1950s, seemed large sums, and from 1957 scholarships ceased to cover the whole tuition fee.

While the Mercers doubted whether the High Master had 'any real conception of the seriousness of the situation', successive High Masters were tempted to see the Mercers as remote, dictatorial and parsimonious. Pre-war memories did not help: the foresight which had set up the Maintenance Fund appeared at the chalk-face, and, especially, on the games field, like meanness. Very small items of expenditure had to be accounted for. Even James, cautious and conservative himself and coolly good-humoured, wrote in measured indignation to the Master in 1952 of a pre-war policy which had forced the games masters, if they were not to run short of footballs and cricket balls, to collect cash directly from the boys. In 1946 Harbord could only get a refrigerator for his boarding house by asking Oakeshott to ask the Governors. James added conciliatorily that in his High Mastership things had become quite different. From 1951 the High Master was given control of ordinary expenditure within the annual budget. But he clearly feared a return to the old ways.

Gilkes recalled those old ways, years after his retirement, with a good deal of bitterness. He thought that the staff in the 1920s had been unhappy, and remembered a whip-round in the Common Room for a long-serving colleague whose pension was too small for him to be able to get home to France. It had been quite different in the 1950s: the Governors were now proud of the School, and he praised, in particular, the Clerk, Colonel Geoffrey Logsden. But Gilkes's relations with Mercers' Hall had sometimes been very strained indeed, especially in 1956 when he thought the masters were being subjected to sharp practice over their pension contributions, and in 1958, when he was infuriated by a decision that a groundsman had to be given priority for accommodation over the Chaplain. Gilkes felt that the Governors were excluding him humiliatingly from important policy decisions, and that the Trustees ought to have control over how much money was spent, but not over how it was spent. He irritated the Governors at their meetings, to which the High Master was now usually invited, by introducing business that was not on the Agenda and by enlisting the support of university governors against Mercers. For all his reserved and patrician exterior, Gilkes was a man of strong passions, and sometimes put pen to paper with dangerous effusiveness. It was possibly understandable that he was not always sure which Watney was which (in 1956 there were six on the governing body), but it was hardly tactful to tell the Clerk.

A deeply religious man, Gilkes was the author of a perceptive early work on the Dead Sea Scrolls. Since the 1930s the daily prayers had been enlivened by hymn singing accompanied by the great 'Father Willis' organ, a memorial to Jowett. Gilkes was open in his liking for Christian commitment in the men he appointed to the staff, and though he considered the Jewish presence in the School 'a source of great strength', he also favoured a statutory minimum of boys of Christian background: in 1960 the Governors fixed this at 85 per cent. This was not only invidious, but difficult to operate effectively. Translated, inevitably though inaccurately, into a 'Jewish quota', it gave much offence, and led to resignations, including Isaiah Berlin's, from the Old Pauline Club. Yet Gilkes, like James, also valued the cosmopolitan and metropolitan atmosphere of the School. Paulines, he thought, excelled at getting on with people of all kinds, because of the less narrow and sheltered lives they led than did boys from conventional public schools. Thus when, towards the end of his High Mastership, the possibility of a move across the river first arose, he was in two minds. He and his predecessor had successfully restored Pauline life on a site which Gilkes had known and, on balance, loved for nearly forty years. 'It was an awfully bad building really', yet, illuminated for the anniversary of 1959, 'it flamed like the last act of *Götterdämmerung*.' In many different ways, and perhaps in schools as much as anywhere, the new decade was indeed to seem like the passing of the old order, the Twilight of the Gods.

*The Great Hall, with the Willis Organ, the figures of St Paul and Colet in mosaic on either side, and the child Jesus above. None of the mosaics came to Barnes. 'We got an expert from Ravenna,' Howarth explained, 'and he took one look at them . . .' But thirty years later the iconoclasm of the 1960s seems puzzling and bleak.*

115

# IX

## 'THE SAME SCHOOL THAT HE STARTED'

*Sir Anthony Jay*

### 1962–1990

Fﾏ ﾏﾏ Hﾏﾏ ﾏﾏ Mﾏﾏﾏﾏﾏﾏﾏ, a high figure in that old order, was a loyal Pauline. In the course of his campaigns he had found time to reply warmly to the congratulations sent him from the School and to send it souvenirs of his victories. He rigorously inspected the School's cadet force in 1944, and in 1956 unveiled a Latin inscription in the Board Room which commemorated his wartime occupation of it. In old age he still welcomed schoolboy visitors from St Paul's to his Hampshire home ('They can wear any old clothes they like. They must get their hair cut.') He was, of course, a Governor of the School.

Among the young officers on Montgomery's staff in the last months of the war was T. E. B. Howarth, a Winchester master and temporary major who had fought in Normandy and north-west Europe, and won the MC. Montgomery took to Howarth at once, and though Howarth described himself as Monty's licensed jester, he was taken seriously enough to be sent to his own former division to find out what was wrong with it and to be given a key part in arranging the German surrender in Schleswig-Holstein. After the war Howarth returned to Winchester, where Montgomery's son David was briefly his pupil. On Gilkes's resignation Montgomery was one of a small committee of head-hunters. Howarth, who by then had had four years as headmaster of King Edward's Birmingham followed

To: The School Staff.

Christmas and New Year
Greetings

From: B. L. Montgomery
General
Eighth Army.

Italy
Xmas 1943

"Tac" H.Q. Eighth Army
C.M.F.

by ten as second master at Winchester, was inevitably Monty's man. Not long after his appointment he was told: 'If you have any trouble with the other governors, ring me up and I'll bring up the heavy artillery.'

It is probable that the big guns were not much needed. Howarth, as courageous as Montgomery, and sometimes almost as ruthless, possessed a more widely appreciated charm and the finesse in which the Field Marshal was so utterly lacking. He had an unashamed love of cleverness and an excellent academic mind himself; he had already published the first and most distinguished of several scholarly books, his life of Louis Philippe, *Citizen King* (1961). For this was not only the first Cambridge High Master since 1769 (and he piqued himself on a Cambridge man's scepticism and short way with cant), it was also the first High Master ever who was not a classicist. To Howarth, Montgomery was '*par excellence*' a teacher, and he may have found his experiences at close quarters with the Field Marshal as

*July 1946: Montgomery scrutinizes his guard of honour. Major A. G. Harbord (Housemaster and commanding officer of the CCF) is on the Field Marshal's right, and High Master Oakeshott a pace or two behind.*

117

valuable a training for the High Mastership as the historical tripos in which he had gained a double first.

Howarth's two successors have also been historians (and Cambridge men). Yet this visible shift in the order of things marked the golden sunset rather than the triumphal dawn of the history department's age of glory. For Andrew Schonfield, in 1934–6 the School had been a penumbra whose bright centre was the History Eighth; for Karl Leyser in 1938 the History Eighth was Whitting. Whitting retired in 1963. In 1964 modern languages, which had been largely ancillary to history, were organized into an autonomous eighth form. The reputation and distinction of the classical teaching were as great as ever; but the numbers in the classical eighth were not. They included some of the cleverest boys, who moved rapidly up the School and specialized early. The Science Eighth was growing fast (from thirty-eight boys in 1952 to seventy-two in 1955) and to Jonathan Miller the biology labs were a civilizing city state.

Yet in the middle years of the century the still scarcely shaken confidence of the English liberal academic élite was reflected in the history department of St Paul's by what to the rest of the School probably appeared irritating complacency and arrogance, and to its members felt like the excitement of an intellectual programme that worked. When the unofficial School newspaper, *Folio*, held a public opinion poll to find 'Mr. Pseudo 1962', 'the élite of the History VIII . . . as expected figures well in the final result'. When the same magazine interviewed the new High Master he felt that history was the best subject to provide the 'humanistic replacement' necessitated by the quantitative decline of classics.

Howarth, though much older when appointed than his three predecessors had been, was not at all displeased to be thought rather an *enfant terrible*. Early in his High Mastership he attacked and destroyed two powerful institutions, boxing and

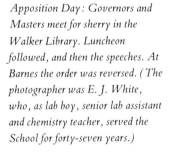

*Apposition Day: Governors and Masters meet for sherry in the Walker Library. Luncheon followed, and then the speeches. At Barnes the order was reversed. (The photographer was E. J. White, who, as lab boy, senior lab assistant and chemistry teacher, served the School for forty-seven years.)*

*Apposition 1965. The Master of the Mercers presents the prizes while, as the High Master remarked: 'The bulldozers are now at work – at Barnes, I mean, not here.'*

the CCF. In 1962 the reputation of boxing at St Paul's was as high as ever. Nicolas Luard of *Private Eye* knew nothing of Paulines except that they were good boxers. He was making the point that public schools were sadistic. It was more serious that in 1963 the Medical Officer expressed his worries to the Governors, serious enough for Howarth to act accordingly. Only two men had run school boxing, both of them legends to the boys they trained – 'Bo' Langham (who had never boxed himself) and 'Buster' Reed, (who never quite recovered from the abolition). The CCF (formerly OTC/JTC) was even more, to the young men of the 1960s, a symbol of all that was dubious about public schools. In 1962 Gilkes reported that it was difficult to find officers among the young masters. Times must have changed since Jonathan Miller had found no lack of 'horrific epitomes of terrible, jingoistic, chauvinistic public schoolism that can pass as masters' at St Paul's, while admitting that there were also an unusual number of first-class brains. Some of the first-class brains were in fact officers of the CCF, and its demolition, though it removed the embarrassment some boys felt in travelling to school in uniform on Mondays, established the new High Master's radical reputation with rather a firm smack.

These changes were insignificant compared to the one which Howarth was really appointed to implement. Although in 1952 the Governors appeared to have firmly settled against moving the School, the depredations of the Talgarth Road, the soaring costs of maintaining the Victorian buildings, and the opportunity, to be seized or lost for ever, of acquiring 40 riverside acres, not too far away and not too expensive, all brought about a change of heart. When Howarth became High Master, the move was probable; by the time he had established himself it was certain. The move to Barnes also crossed the Rubicon of his regime, and the young man in a hurry had become, south of the Thames, the still brisk and mercurial champion of Pauline values against a brave new world.

At the end of his High Mastership, Howarth recalled the excitement of discussion with the architect, Bernard Fielden, out of which a new school took shape – or rather shape after ingenious shape, as the geometric patterns gave place to each other on the drawing-board. 'A century ago', said Fielden in 1965, 'architects were purveyors of style; today we are purveyors of utility and environment.' This was unjust to Waterhouse, who had also tried to put the needs of the customer first. As it turned out, Fielden's building, just as much as Waterhouse's, was constrained by economics as well as geography; as to style, it is true there was none: 'We are plunging into a social and technical chaos', he went on, 'and trying to discover the right answer.'

Howarth took the plunge. The new School, built on former waterworks' filter-beds, has an enormous swimming pool and no Assembly Hall. In 1969 he was to observe that it was of the highest importance that any building where the whole School could assemble should not exist. This was to make a virtue of a decision at least partly dictated by financial stringency. But it was in tune with Howarth's personality: brilliant as lecturer or conversationalist, he hated, as he put it, bringing down the tablets from Sinai, and doubted the wisdom of struggling on with compulsory morning prayers for all. Instead, a theatre provided floor space for prayers

*May 1969: the Lord Mayor of London opens the new School, which had in fact been functioning for two terms. He described the principles of the School (and of the City of London) as 'fair dealing, honest conduct, tolerance, and hard work'.*

*Variegated icons, of Jowett, Colet and Edward Thomas, preside over industrious Paulines in the Library.*

for juniors, and a chapel, rather bare and small, to suit the religious expectations of the 1960s, was to be used for voluntary worship. It probably amounted to the right bundle of decisions, though it contained a mechanical cuckoo, indestructible and detested by all – the tannoy.

A central library, accessible, unlike the old Walker Library, to boys of all ages, classrooms organized departmentally, with departmental study-centres, science laboratories adequate in space and equipment and not isolated from the rest of the School, living space for boys including common-rooms, individual study cubicles (carrels) for eighth-formers, diversified provision for games – all these were attempted, and at least partially achieved. The sports complex was, and still is, a show-piece, and the more necessary in the early years at Barnes, because the playing fields were inadequately drained and thickly strewn with stones. But the grounds were improved, and the starkness of the buildings relieved, by an excellent head groundsman and a generous policy of tree-planting.

The boys' common-rooms, Howarth ruefully observed, were little used: they were soon to be depleted, anyhow, by pressing need for more classrooms. Since the war the whole School, instead of less than half of it, ate lunch on site, so that a canteen made obvious sense if the long midday break was to be well used. So did the carpets in corridors and classrooms, which greatly excited the press, but are tough, necessary noise-reducers, and not very glamorous. The Library, an elegant and attractive room, did form something of the civilizing centre hoped for. But, like much else, it was, almost from the beginning, too small – and numbers continued to grow.

*'And there stydyed upon there books, every one in his carrell all the after none.'*

As early as 1961, when the move was still far from certain, it had been decided that the Girls' School would not come too. There has consequently been only one female Pauline in 480 years, the daughter of a former Chaplain, who spent a term, rather unofficially, in the History Eighth. Despite dances, drama, music, some senior seminars and a converging governing body, the schools have remained their separate selves. Colet Court did come, but remained in practice very much a separate school at its other end of the campus, its headmasters never again so obviously subordinates as in the years immediately following its annexation.

The move appeared to a very junior master to occur with effortless smoothness. In July 1968 we went home from Hammersmith: in September we came back to Barnes. There were parties of Old Paulines to be shown round the building: we tended to get lost while doing this. Thus the School got on with being 'the same school that he [Colet] started'. This was Howarth's real triumph. In fact, of course, not only was the move itself complex and difficult: the years of preparation were much more so. Local authorities moved slowly to grant the necessary permissions, building costs rose – from an estimated £1 million pounds in February 1965 to £1,800,000 in June – and the sale of the Gunnersbury land was much less profitable than expected. At one point it looked as though one boarding house would have to be given up or High House would have to stay in Hammersmith. An appeal was necessary, for £500,000; of this the Mercers' Company gave £100,000, over and above the £137,000 already contributed by the Colet Trust. The huge financial decisions that the Mercers had to take, Howarth thought, drew them much closer to the School: and he rightly considered that the much improved relations that he established with the Governors were one of the most important achievements of his High Mastership. Secure in their confidence, he was able to orchestrate with apparent calm control a performance very far from effortless. Meanwhile, as a potentially hostile 'youth-culture' and a major political attack on public schools surged around him, the High Master, though not noticeably less sardonic or sceptical, had become the champion of the Pauline household gods.

Not, however, of their images. Of these, few crossed the Thames. Montgomery was said to have suggested that the only essentials were the portraits of himself and Marlborough. Haimo Thorneycroft's fine statue of Colet came, and Torrigiano's bust, and a very little stained glass. The mosaics in the Great Hall were sold off; some of the glass briefly graced a Kensington emporium. Like Erasmus, with whom he had much else in common, Howarth found civilized values almost entirely in the written and spoken word, and with this he was fighting *contra mundum*. On the Newsome Commission on Public Schools, as token and supposedly leftish headmaster, he signed, with two others, a note of dissent which pointed out and repudiated the destruction of academic standards, as well as independence, involved in the main commission's proposals. His *Culture, Anarchy and the Public Schools* (1969) was an early shot in the counter-attack againt the then dominant consensus of the educational left. In the same year, its centenary year, he served as Chairman of the Headmasters' Conference.

In Howarth's first two years there were unusually numerous changes among the junior masters. He was to look back on his early, adventurous, appointments as 'disastrous'. Few lasted long, and those who followed were more conventional,

*The statue of Colet with two boys was given by a Governor, Mr E. H. Palmer, and unveiled in 1902. In 1985 Mrs Joan Newman wrote to the High Master: her father, when a child, had been the model for the two boys; might she bring her grandchildren to see them?*

*Hammersmith rowers had to set out from a boat-house on the wrong side of the Broadway; now the river is on the School's doorstep. A new and much more spacious boathouse, just downstream of the boarding houses, was opened in 1973.*

among them a former Wykehamist pupil who is now a Lefebvrist bishop. The most obvious shift to the right was the appointment in 1964 of F. G. Commings to succeed the beloved and omnicompetent A. B. Cook as Surmaster.

Commings was a man of formidable dedication and directness, the epitome of Pauline qualities as seen by their admirers and their critics. He cannot have enjoyed the Feast Sermon of 1970 'On Being a Real Person', which began by discussing *The Naked Ape* (1967), a book not then allowed in the School Library. For a time he and Howarth found it hard to bear each other, especially as Commings thought the High Master was allowing discipline to slide and Howarth thought that Commings treated as moral problems what were merely changes in fashion. But the hard work of the move drew them together, and so did Howarth's growing disillusionment with the idols of the era. In 1969, when he had to order several expulsions because of drug-taking, Howarth was visibly and deeply shocked; it was Commings who could take comfort in a boy's reply to a reporter nosing for dirt: 'It's a bloody good school. It's a pity just a few want to spoil it.' Somehow, with the help of a staff that included rather a lot of very young men and several very sane and unflappable older ones, they pulled the School fairly happily through the years of 'youthquake'. The boarding houses, whose future had often seemed precarious before the move, now grew and flourished under housemasters who could provide centres of continuity and community: in identical buildings next to each other on the river bank they retained their separate identities, though not the tradition that School House was for weekly boarders and High House for hearties who stayed through the weekend.

Howarth's involvement in the strategy of the move and in high educational politics meant that more day-to-day management was delegated than before. All modern Surmasters have been overworked, even though offices have proliferated, an Assistant Bursar being appointed to manage part of the financial business of the move, and retained (and even, for a time, duplicated) afterwards, and in 1966 an Undermaster for disciplinary and administrative chores. That two Undermasters were found necessary from 1974, and three from 1988, would perhaps amuse, perhaps worry, the Old Pauline author of *Corporation Man* (1971), Sir Anthony Jay, but was no doubt justified by the growing complexity of the curriculum, and the consequent need to advise very young boys faced with difficult choices.

It was Jay who, when Tom Howarth left St Paul's in 1973 to be Senior Tutor of Magdalene College, Cambridge, seized upon the unusual opportunity to interview on film four living and lively ex-High Masters. 'Which is the real Tom Howarth,' he asked, 'the reactionary or the revolutionary?' No one who knew Tom would have expected a simple answer – or have been surprised by the simple utter conviction with which, a few moments later, he denied Jay's hint that a part of him had resisted the School's 'great absorptive powers'. 'No, I wouldn't accept that. I'm absolutely devoted to the place.'

The fleeting and marginal appearance in the film of a fifth High Master, designate but not yet installed, was appropriate to a man whose low profile was anything but an affectation of modesty. Warwick Hele had been known as a courageous cross-country runner at a tough school (Sedbergh), had served in the war, had got a first at Cambridge and run a house at Rugby, where he was also second master. He came to St Paul's with a reputation as a disciplinarian; some senior boys, and possibly some junior masters, thought that there was now a High Master of the conventional kind against whom they could enjoy conventional grievances. The use of Christian names on reports was discouraged. It was rumoured, wrongly, that the CCF and boxing would be revived. This looked like a less epigrammatic, more conventional, era.

*Caelum non animum mutant qui trans mare currunt* – sea changes don't transmute the soul – true of people, less certain of institutions. It is not difficult to guess at the thinking of the Governors. They needed a man who would ensure, once again, that the essence of St Paul's survived uprooting; they needed a consolidator. Utterly different, and not only in style, from his predecessor, Hele made no dramatic reversals; his conservatism was, after all, not far removed from the later Howarth's: they were equally uninterested in up-to-date educational philosophy. In language which Howarth would not have used, but would not have repudiated, Hele could speak convincingly, because sincerely, of 'old-fashioned virtues like service, self-discipline and duty'. Undemonstrative, rather diffident in social

*Four High Masters meet to honour the retiring Surmaster in the Board Room, July 1964. From left to right: R. L. James (then headmaster of Harrow), A. N. Gilkes (then Director of the Public Schools Appointments Bureau), A. B. Cook, T. E. B. Howarth, and W. F. Oakeshott (then Rector of Lincoln College, Oxford).*

approach, he was in fact enormously kind-hearted, pitilessly demanding only to himself.

He regarded the High Mastership as the summit of a schoolmaster's career, rightly thinking of himself as better suited to St Paul's than to Charterhouse. Hints of the possibility of a more glamorous appointment a few years later had no appeal to him. Nor did the colourful showmanship practised by the headmaster a few miles down the river. Television cameras were not welcome at St Paul's, and, unlike his predecessor, Hele seldom wrote to *The Times*.

When he did write, it was on questions of curriculum. By now the pressures for curricular change were powerful, complex and contradictory – utilitarian as well as egalitarian. When, in 1973–4, St Paul's won thirty-six open awards at Oxford and Cambridge, there was gratified debate over whether this was the best year ever; but ten years later, the old system of entrance examinations had been abolished at both universities, and this killed the Upper Eighth, and an exciting and valuable term for many Pauline boys and masters. As the top of the School shrank, its bottom broadened. The same year, 1984, also saw the end of the two-year sprint to O levels, which St Paul's was one of the last schools to retain. But the old order was also threatened by market forces both parental and national: the very success of Howarth's appeal to middle-class aspirations against 'Edmass' means that the values of a liberal education have to compete in a rather chilly market-place with those of an extended management training course.

Most Paulines and their parents, however, seemed content with the fairly traditional teaching and range of subjects which St Paul's continued to offer. Hele was instrumental in fighting off some of the early attempts to emasculate A levels. He was an early supporter of the AS level scheme, which offers a promising combination of rigour and breadth. Within the School he set in motion an exhausting overhaul of the lower school curriculum: committees and fly-sheets proliferated; and just as the infant scheme began to toddle, GCSE slaughtered it. All the same, the exercise had familiarized everybody with the new facts of life, with Computer Studies and CDT, with pressures for ever more elaborate permutations of curricular choice even for the younger boys.

There were more of these boys: in the 1970s numbers rose from about 670 to (for a short time) a peak of 780. Not everyone was happy about this. It was difficult to extend accommodation, not only because of expense but because of the site's status as Open Space. But it was also difficult to reject applicants who reached a standard in Common Entrance which many preparatory schools regarded as swingeingly high. Besides, Hele hated to refuse a Pauline education to anybody who could obviously benefit from it. He quietly dropped the 'Jewish quota', thus healing old wounds, and enthusiastically welcomed the Assisted Places Scheme, even though, as he came ruefully to recognize, it did not bring in as many working-class boys as had been hoped. Numbers of masters (of whom by 1985 four were mistresses) kept up. The Governors were quick to respond to housing problems by acquiring nearby property for young staff: the staff was, however, rather stable, and consequently rather more middle-aged in 1985 than in 1965, partly because people enjoyed life at St Paul's, partly because promotions to head-masterships were rare.

Hele's relations with the Governors were as good as Howarth's had been: one of them called him the best headmaster in England. He was happier dealing with individuals than groups. This was true of his contacts with both staff and parents, and neither he nor the Governors were prepared to welcome a formal parents' organization which wanted an entrée to the financial as well as the educational policy of the School. Hele preferred to foster relations with parents via the tutorial system, and he urged parents and tutors to get to know one another socially. Organized visits of parents to the School did grow, and have grown more under Hele's successor, who is friendlier to the idea of a parent–teacher association. Open Day, the most artificial and exhausting of these meetings, however, disappeared in 1989, to the audible relief of some, leaving the field to Apposition, which had been revived in quasi-traditional form, rather in the manner of a nineteenth-century jousting-match, by Howarth twenty years earlier.

In these modern Appositions a Governor from one of the universities is asked to animadvert on several public, usually prize-winning, performances. In 1989 these included a summary of an essay on particle physics, which had won the BP Research International Physics Prize, and a discussion of new developments in con-

*Sketching the Laocöon. 'Wandering up to the first floor I found it pleasantly flooded with the afternoon sun. . . In the middle of the corridor, perched on a stool, was a fair-sized swarthy boy drawing at an easel. I recognised in this phenomenon one, Kennington, who lived not as other men, but like a bird, rather, on a perch, knocking off likenesses of the plaster casts and whistling tunelessly the while.' (Paul Nash,* An Autobiography, *1949.)*

tact lens design, by a boy whose work in that field had already enabled him to launch a successful business venture. There is almost always a musical piece, and often something from the visual arts.

The increased attention to these is, of course, not particularly Pauline, any more than the remark in a *Pauline* of the early twentieth century that art could never hope to be a major element in public school life had been. In those days art was mainly a matter of accurate drawing, and its study was awarded as a punishment or an alternative to prayers; hence the description of the Art School as 'a synagogue in the morning and a penitentiary in the afternoon'. The Barnes buildings attempted to house both art and music amply, though it was soon discovered that only the Sports Hall was big enough for major musical occasions. Drama, though its Pauline connexions go back almost to the beginning of the School, was at first less happily provided for at Barnes: a successful transformation of the very inadequate Theatre was one of the last achievements of Hele's High Mastership. He carried out an equally successful transformation of the Chapel, and it was he, and not Howarth, the sometime critic of compulsory worship, who agreed to abandon compulsory chapel for boarders on Sundays. Morning assembly, already only required for Juniors, was soon afterwards excused sixth-formers, and cut to three days a week.

*The Caucasian Chalk Circle, junior play, March 1989, performed by fourth- and fifth-formers, with girls from Godolphin and Latymer School. The new theatre was opened by Jonathan Miller in 1987.*

*The Chesterton (Junior Debating) Society in session, 1989, in the Montgomery Room. The map used to plan the invasion of Normandy is on the far wall. Behind the young orator can be seen (left to right) portraits of High Masters Bell, Hillard and Hele.*

*The Art Department in action: raku firing, 1988.*

Nowadays assembly may be devoted to a talk about *A Brief History of Time* by an agnostic master or a ten-minute morality play by three prefects. Some masters attend; none wear gowns, there or anywhere else. The stately entry of Gilkes, heralded by the even more stately Searle, the frock-coated Head Porter, jangling his keys for silence, the High Master's 'Oremus', the Latin Prayers read by the Captain of the School, all seem infinitely remote. They had already seemed frigidly irrelevant to R. S. Baldock, who, as a boy in the Upper Eighth, wrote to *Folio* about them in 1962. In 1984 Baldock succeeded P. F. Thomson as Surmaster. Thomson, who knew, it seemed, every boy in the School, and the right college or university for most of them, kept a permanently open study door, except when away with the Lower Eighth Historians, inspecting the Anglo-Saxon churches of Sussex and Hampshire. He was a committee man only perforce. Baldock, the seventeenth Old Pauline to hold the Surmastership, came to it after seven years as Housemaster of School House. When, two years later, Hele retired from the High Mastership, though not from the high politics of education, his successor, a man of wholly different style, was quick to recognize the efficiency of the School's administration, and that Baldock was the latest of a line of strong and competent Surmasters.

'Most headmasters talk a lot', remarked Peter Pilkington the other day. A good talker himself, he was the close friend of two famous conversationalists, Howarth and his friend the economist, John Vaizey, who allied with Howarth on the Newsome Commission, and sent his sons to St Paul's. The first *mot* of Pilkington's to reach the School was his cheerful warning to his former school, King's Canterbury, that 'lame ducks can still bite'. One rumour had been that the new High Master would come from industry or commerce, worlds whose techniques and styles, and values too, are knocking loud on the classroom door. Instead came somebody who looks very traditional indeed: professional schoolmaster (who had ruled College at Eton), clergyman (very High Church, he immediately ordered the Chaplain to buy a censer), historian (much given to the Tudors and Stuarts).

That was the image: the reality is for a future historian to judge. But it is not quite, perhaps not at all, what it might seem. This short, energetic, smiling, highly articulate man believes that what needs to be done can be done. He describes himself as a pragmatist, conscious, of course, of the paradox, for his Christianity is credally dogmatic, but conscious too that he is piloting a school founded in the ideals of Christian humanism through a world of no fixed ideals. He intends that St Paul's shall compete successfully with any great school in the country, and doubts if that is compatible with low fees: it certainly means building, which he has already begun to do. He believes it must relate to social and educational change, and that it may have to change fast if it is to keep the initiative. He consults his staff, as a group, much more than his predecessors did: but he takes the decisions himself. He wants to pay his staff better and to demand more of them. He wants more language teaching, more choral music, more prep schools to send their best boys to St Paul's. The future is, he suspects, a foreign country; they do things differently there, and we had better learn their ways. Yet he also wants, I think, St Paul's still to be the same school that that other clergyman founded, that very different clergyman who was also a radical and a conservative, a pragmatist and an idealist, and put his trust in God and a City Company.

It would not be difficult to draw up an impressive list of Pauline achievement in the 1970s and 1980s. It could range from traditional academic success to the organization of charitable marathons via an almost monotonous series of triumphs in bridge and chess: in 1982 St Paul's won the *Daily Mail* Bridge Cup and *The Times* Chess Tournament. It also won the Youll Cup five years running: tennis is a good vehicle for what Paulines like to think of as the Pauline qualities of mental agility, physical rigour and individual competitiveness. But a history has no business to be a prospectus; any good school can list such achievements, and no such lists brings us much closer to the *Res Paulina*, the suchness of our School, its soul. Has it a soul? 'Is there a theme?' a friend of mine asked, in one of many useful conversations I had with him while writing this book. Could he have remembered, perhaps, a regrettable fondness, expounded at him when he was an eighth-former, for the view that 'history is just one damned thing after another'? Schoolmasters like to imagine that their teaching is remembered. 'I don't think so,' I replied, playing it in character, 'except that institutions are good at surviving.' 'Wasn't there a motto?' asked my friend, innocently. 'Of course there was', said the pedant, falling into the trap. 'Don't you remember, on the badge on your blazer? *Fide et Literis*, Faith and Letters?'

It has always been hard to translate, and it is getting harder. My friend is a rather liberal Jew: I am a rather orthodox Christian. We know quite well that history is not just one damned thing after another. St Paul's is not just a successful institution for advancing the careers of the middle classes. If it were, its history would not be worth writing. It has always had, please God it always will have, sons and servants who have tried to live and to teach *fide et literis*. 'The wise and sagacious Founder,' wrote Erasmus, 'saw that the greatest Hopes and Happiness of the Commonwealth were in the training up of Children to good letters and true Religion.' Amen. *Floreat Schola Paulina.*

'*But let my due feet never fail
To walk the studious cloister's pale.*'
(*Milton*)

# SELECTED LIST OF OLD PAULINES

* indicates those who were probably, but not certainly, Paulines.

THOMAS LUPSET *c.* 1495–1530. Scholar; Prebendary of Salisbury.

EDWARD NORTH, 1st Lord North, 1496–1564. Privy Counsellor.

ROBERT PURSGLOVE *c.* 1500–1571. Last Prior of Guisborough; Bishop Suffragan of Hull.

JOHN CLEMENT *c.* 1500–1572. Reader in Greek at Oxford University; President of the College of Physicians; tutor to the children of Sir Thomas More.

ANTHONY DENNY 1501–1549. Privy Counsellor; Groom of the Stool.

THOMAS WRIOTHESLEY, 1st Earl of Southampton, *c.* 1505–1550. KG; Lord Chancellor.

WILLIAM PAGET, 1st Lord Paget, 1505–1563. KG; Secretary of State; Lord Privy Seal.

JOHN LELAND *c.* 1506–1552. Antiquary.

*JOHN MORE *c.* 1508–1547. Youngest son of Sir Thomas More and imprisoned with him in the Tower.

GEORGE LILY *c.* 1512–1559. Son of the first High Master; Chaplain to Cardinal Pole.

THOMAS GRESHAM *c.* 1518–1579. Ambassador to the Netherlands; founder of the Royal Exchange.

*THOMAS TUSSER *c.* 1524–1580. Author of *Five Hundred Good Points of Husbandrie etc.*

WILLIAM HARRISON 1534–1593. Author of *A Description of England.*

WILLIAM FULKE 1538–1589. Puritan divine; Master of Pembroke College, Cambridge; Vice-Chancellor of Cambridge University.

*EDMUND CAMPION 1540–1581. Jesuit martyr; canonized 1970.

ROBERT LANEHAM *flor.* 1540. Traveller, musician and drinker.

WILLIAM WHITAKER 1547–1595. Theologian; Master of St John's College, Cambridge; Regius Professor of Divinity, Cambridge.

WILLIAM CAMDEN 1551–1623. Antiquary; Headmaster of Westminster; Clarenceux King-of-Arms.

BAPTIST HICKS, 1st Viscount Campden, 1551–1629. Master of the Mercers' Company; founder of the Campden Exhibitions.

JOHN HOWSON *c.* 1556–1632. Bishop of Durham.

FRANCIS VERE 1560–1609. General.

THOMAS MUDDE c. 1560–c. 1619. Musician.

JOHN SANDERSON 1560–c. 1622. Traveller and diplomat.

RICHARD CLERKE c. 1560–1634. One of the translators of the Authorized Version.

JOHN BOYLE 1564–1620. Bishop of Cork.

RICHARD BOYLE c. 1570–1645. Archbishop of Tuam.

LIONEL CRANFIELD, 1st Earl of Middlesex, 1575–1645. Lord Treasurer.

NATHAN FIELD 1587–c. 1633. Playwright and actor.

*THOMAS RAVENSCROFT 1592–c. 1635. Composer.

BARTON HOLLIDAIE 1593–1661. Chaplain to Charles I; author of *Technogamia, or the Marriage of the Arts, a comedie*, which bored James I in 1621.

ALEXANDER GILL 1597–1644. High Master.

ROGER TWYSDEN, 2nd Baronet, 1597–1672. Diarist, antiquarian, ecclesiastical controversialist.

JOHN MILTON 1608–1674. Poet.

THOMAS HORTON 1609–1673. President of Queens' College, Cambridge; Vice-Chancellor of Cambridge University.

CHRISTOPHER MILTON 1615–1693. Chief Justice of the Common Pleas.

CHARLES SCARBOROUGH 1615–1694. FRS; MP; MD; Physician to Charles II, James II and William III.

NATHANIEL CULVERWELL c. 1619–1651. Fellow of Emmanuel College, Cambridge; one of the Cambridge Platonists.

THANKFULL OWEN 1620–1681. President of St John's College, Oxford.

THOMAS SMITH 1624–1661. Cambridge University Librarian.

PETER PETT 1630–1699. Fellow of All Souls College, Oxford; FRS; Advocate General for Ireland.

THOMAS DAVIES 1631–1680. Lord Mayor of London.

RICHARD CUMBERLAND 1631–1718. Bishop of Peterborough.

RICHARD MEGGOTT c. 1632–1692. Dean of Winchester.

JOHN WAGSTAFFE 1633–1677. Author of *Historical reflections on the Bishop of Rome* and *The Question of Witchcraft debated* (he disbelieved in it).

SAMUEL PEPYS 1633–1703. Diarist; Secretary to the Admiralty; President of the Royal Society.

JOHN TREVOR 1637–1717. Speaker of the House of Commons, 1685, 1690–5; expelled from the House of Commons for taking bribes 1695; Master of the Rolls 1685, 1697–1717.

HUMPHREY GOWER c. 1638–1711. Master of St John's College, Cambridge; Lady Margaret Professor of Divinity; Vice-Chancellor of Cambridge University.

GEORGE VINER, 2nd Baronet, 1639–1673. 'Very civil' to Pepys, who called his wife 'almost the finest woman that I ever saw'.

*WILLIAM WYCHERLEY 1640–1716. Playwright.

GEORGE HOOPER 1640–1727. Bishop of St Asaph; Bishop of Bath and Wells.

BENJAMIN CALAMY 1642–1686. Chaplain to Charles II; friend of Judge Jeffreys; preacher against Nonconformity.

JOHN STRYPE 1643–1737. Antiquarian and biographer.

GEORGE JEFFREYS, 1st Baron Jeffreys, 1648–1689. Lord Chief Justice (of the Bloody Assize); Lord Chancellor.

SAMUEL JOHNSON 1649–1703. Controversial writer; fined, pilloried and whipped for writing against James II; pensioned by William III.

JOHN CHURCHILL, 1st Duke of Marlborough, 1650–1722. Captain-General; Prince of the Holy Roman Empire.

EDWARD NORTHEY 1652–1723. Attorney-General.

SAMUEL BRADFORD 1652–1731. Bishop of Rochester; Dean of Westminster.

RALPH GREY, 4th Lord Grey of Warke, c. 1656–1706. Governor of Barbados.

ROBERT NELSON 1656–1715. Non-juror; author of *Festivals and Fasts of the Church of England*.

EDMOND HALLEY 1656–1742. Astronomer Royal.

PHILIP AYSCOUGH *c.* 1657–1742. High Master.

GEORGE DODINGTON *c.* 1658–1720. MP; Secretary to the Commissioners for Union with Scotland 1706; Treasurer of the Navy; Lord Lieutenant of Somersetshire.

CHARLES MONTAGU, 4th Earl and 1st Duke of Manchester, *c.* 1660–1722. Ambassador to Venice, France and Austria; Secretary of State.

CHARLES PEERS *c.* 1660–1737. Lord Mayor of London; Master of the Salters' Company.

WILLIAM NICHOLS 1664–1711. Canon of Chichester; author of a commentary on the Prayer Book; preacher at the Feast 1698.

JAMES STANLEY, 10th Earl of Derby, 1664–1736. Chancellor of the Duchy of Lancaster; Captain of the Yeomen of the Guard.

FRANCIS MARSH *c.* 1665–1693. Dean of Down.

JOHN LENG 1665–1727. Bishop of Norwich.

ROBERT STEPHENS 1665–1732. Historiographer Royal.

EDWARD GIBBON 1666–1737. Financial speculator; director of the South Sea Company; property confiscated after the Bubble; made a second fortune; grandfather of the historian.

WILLIAM GRIGG 1667–1720. Master of Clare College, Cambridge; Vice-Chancellor of the University.

ANTHONY HAMMOND 1668–1739. Duellist; MP for Cambridge University; Commissioner of the Navy.

SPENCER COWPER 1669–1728. Judge.

NATHANIEL LLOYD 1669–1741. Dean of the Arches; Master of Trinity Hall, Cambridge; Vice-Chancellor of Cambridge.

WILLIAM LEGGE, 1st Earl of Dartmouth, 1672–1750. Secretary of State; Lord Privy Seal.

ROBERT BAYLIS 1673–1748. Lord Mayor of London.

CHARLES BOYLE, 4th Earl of Orrery, 1674–1731. KT; FRS; Privy Counsellor; fought at Malplaquet; Lord of the Bedchamber to George I; imprisoned for Jacobitism.

ROGER GALE 1675–1744. MP; Commissioner of Excise; FRS; treasurer of the Royal Society; first vice-president of the Society of Antiquaries.

SPENCER COMPTON, 1st Earl of Wilmington, 1674–1743. Speaker of the House of Commons; First Lord of the Treasury.

SAMUEL KNIGHT 1678–1746. Biographer of Colet; Archdeacon of Berkshire.

JAMES DORMER 1679–1741. Lieutenant-General; governor of Hull.

ROGER COTES 1782–1716. Fellow of Trinity College, Cambridge, first Plumian Professor of Experimental Philosophy; FRS. (Newton: 'Had Cotes lived, we should have known something.')

ALGERNON COOTE, 6th Earl of Mountrath, 1683–1770. MP; governor of Queen's County, Ireland.

MATTHIAS MAWSON 1683–1770. Bishop of Llandaff, Chichester and Ely.

MARK ANTHONY CORBIERE *c.* 1688–1743. Ambassador to Morroco; commissioner for licences for wine.

RICHARD RAWLINSON 1690–1755. Non-juring bishop.

PEREGRINE OSBORNE, 3rd Duke of Leeds, 1691–1731.

ARCHIBALD DOUGLAS, 2nd Earl of Furfar, 1692–1715. Major-General; ambassador to Prussia; died of wounds in the Jacobite rebellion.

GEORGE MORTON PITT 1693–1756. Governor of Fort St George, Madras.

LACY RYAN *c.* 1694–1760. Actor; author of *The Cobler's Opera* [*sic*]; shot and robbed by a footpad in Great Queen Street, 1735.

★MAURICE GREEN 1695–1755. Organist and composer to the Chapel Royal; Professor of Music at Cambridge University.

GEORGE DANCE *c.* 1695–1768. Architect; designed the Mansion House, London.

ALURED CLARKE 1696–1742. Dean of Exeter.

JOHN STRANGE 1696–1754. Solicitor-General; Master of the Rolls.

TIMOTHY CRUMPE *c.* 1700–1737. High Master.

GEORGE NORTH 1707–1772. Antiquary and numismatist.

WILLIAM BOYCE 1710–1779. Composer, organist of the Chapel Royal.

THOMAS SALMON *c.* 1715–1759. Bishop of Ferns.

JOHN RIVINGTON 1720–1792. Publisher.

★JOHN DOUGLAS 1721–1807. Bishop of Carlisle; Dean of Windsor; Bishop of Salisbury.

JOHN CAMPBELL, 5th Duke of Argyll, 1723–1806. Field Marshal.

LORD FREDERICK CAMPBELL, 1729–1816. Chief Secretary of Ireland.

RICHARD ROBERTS *c.* 1729–1823. High Master.

WILLIAM HAWES *c.* 1736–1808. Founder of the Royal Humane Society.

PHILIP ROSENHAGEN *c.* 1737–1798. Fellow of St John's College, Cambridge; shady clergyman; man of fashion; Archdeacon of Colombo, Ceylon.

PHILIP FRANCIS 1740–1818. Statesman; reputed author of *Junius's Letters.*

WILLIAM GEORGE DIGGES LA TOUCHE 1747–1803. 'No man ever deserved better at the hands of the Arabs, or was more highly respected and esteemed among them than Mr La Touche.'

JOHN FISHER *c.* 1748–1825. Bishop of Exeter; Bishop of Salisbury.

JOHN ANDRÉ *c.* 1751–1780. Brigade-Major; hanged as a spy by the Americans; reburied in Westminster Abbey.

SOLDEN LAWRENCE 1752–1814. Judge.

JOHN GARNETT 1754–1813. Dean of Exeter.

FREDERICK THESIGER 1758–1805. ADC to Nelson; Captain in the Royal and Russian navies.

GEORGE THICKNESSE, 19th Lord Audley, 1758–1805. Nephew of the High Master; was bequeathed his father's right hand as a reminder of his failure in filial duty.

THOMAS TROUBRIDGE, 1st Baronet, *c.*1758–1807. Rear-Admiral; fought at Cape St Vincent and the Nile; lost at sea in the Indian Ocean.

THOMAS CLARKSON 1760–1846. Campaigner against the Slave Trade.

THOMAS EDLYNE TOMLINS 1762–1841. Chancellor of the Exchequer for Ireland.

CHARLES WETHERELL 1770–1846. KC; Attorney-General.

WILLIAM JOBBINS *c.* 1771–1790. Hanged at Tyburn for arson and robbery, aged nineteen (see Newgate Calendar, 20 November 1790).

GEORGE HALL 1771–1843. Master of Pembroke College; Vice-Chancellor of Oxford.

WILLIAM JULIAN 1773–1841. Judge Advocate-General.

ROBERT WILLIAM ELLISTON 1774–1831. Actor, of whom Charles Lamb wrote: 'For thee the Pauline muses weep.'

JOSEPH HALLETT BATTEN *c.* 1778–1837. Principal of the East India Company's College at Haileybury.

THOMAS WILDE, 1st Lord Truro, 1782–1855. Lord Chancellor.

JONATHAN FREDERICK POLLOCK 1783–1870. Lord Chief Baron of the Exchequer.

JAMES DOWLING 1787–1844. Chief Justice of New South Wales.

RICHARD HARRIS BARHAM 1788–1845. 'Thomas Ingoldsby', author of *The Jackdaw of Rheims.*

JOHN HAMILTON REYNOLDS 1796–1852. Poet; friend of Keats.

ALFRED OLLIVANT 1798–1882. Regius Professor of Divinity at Cambridge; Bishop of Llandaff; first president of the Old Pauline Club.

CHRISTOPHER HEATH *c.* 1802–1876. Angel of the Irvingite Church.

LUCIUS BENTINCK CARY, 10th Viscount Falkland, 1803–1884. Governor of Bombay; Captain of the Yeomen of the Guard.

JAMES PRINCE LEE 1804–1869. Headmaster of King Edward's School, Birmingham; first Bishop of Manchester.

FREDERICK JAMES HALLIDAY 1806–1901. Lieutenant-Governor of Bengal.

JOSEPH WILLIAMS BLAKESLEY 1808–1885. Dean of Lincoln; Master of the Mercers' Company.

WILLIAM FREDERICK POLLOCK, 2nd Baronet, 1815–1888. Queen's Remembrancer.

BENJAMIN JOWETT 1817–1893. Master of Balliol College, Oxford; Regius Professor of Greek.

CHARLES RICHARD ALFORD *c.* 1817–1898. Bishop of Victoria (Hong Kong).

JAMES HANNEN, 1st Lord Hannen, *c.* 1821–1894. Lord of Appeal in Ordinary.

ALFRED JAMES CARVER 1826–1909. Surmaster; Master of Dulwich.

CHARLES JOHN CLAY 1827–1905. Printer to the University of Cambridge.

JAMES PRENDERGAST 1828–1921. Chief Justice of New Zealand.

GEORGE FRANCIS POPHAM BLYTH *c.* 1833–1914. Archdeacon of Rangoon 1880; Bishop of Jerusalem 1887.

JOSEPH LEYCESTER LYNE 1837–1908. Father Ignatius, the Monk of Llanthony.

HARRY ESCOMBE 1838–1899. Prime Minister of Natal.

MONTAGU CLEMENTI 1839–1919. Judge Advocate-General, India; Master of the Mercers' Company.

WALTER JOHN LAWRANCE 1840–1914. Dean of St Alban's.

CHARLES JOHN RIDGEWAY 1841–1927. Bishop of Chichester.

JOSEPH WEST RIDGEWAY 1844–1930. Governor of the Isle of Man; Governor of Ceylon.

EDWIN RAY LANKESTER 1847–1929. FRS; zoologist; Professor of Zoology, University College, London; Linacre Professor, Oxford; Curator of the Natural History Museum, London; President of the British Association.

EDMUND ARBUTHNOTT KNOX 1847–1937. Bishop of Manchester.

ALFRED BRAY KEMPE 1849–1922. Chancellor of the Diocese of London; Treasurer and Vice-President of the Royal Society.

FREDERIC WALLIS 1853–1928. Bishop of Wellington, New Zealand.

ARTHUR ERNEST COWLEY 1861–1931. Bodley's Librarian.

SANDFORD ARTHUR STRONG 1863–1904. Librarian to the House of Lords; Professor of Arabic, University College, London.

BERTRAND DAWSON, 1st Viscount Dawson of Penn, 1864–1945. Physician to George V.

FREDERICK WILLIAM HALL 1867–1933. Classical scholar; President of St John's College, Oxford.

ROBERT WILLIAM HAMILTON 1867–1933. President, Court of Appeal, East Africa.

SYDNEY CARLYLE COCKERELL 1867–1962. Director of the Fitzwilliam Museum, Cambridge.

ROBERT LAWRENCE BINYON 1869–1943. Poet.

HERBERT NEWELL BATE 1871–1941. Dean of York.

JAMES BENNETT BRUNYATE 1871–1951. Financial Secretary to the government of India.

CYRIL BAILEY 1871–1957. Classical scholar; Public Orator at Oxford.

LAURIE MAGNUS 1872–1933. Writer.

KIRSOPP LAKE 1872–1946. New Testament scholar.

SRI AUROBINDO (A. A. Ghose) 1872–1952. Sage.

ARTHUR HENRY FROOM 1873–1964. Member of the Council of State for India.

VICTOR MURRAY TROTTER 1874–1929. Judge of the Supreme Court, Madras; Chief Justice.

GILBERT KEITH CHESTERTON 1874–1936. Poet, novelist and artist.

FRANCIS MACDONALD CORNFORD 1874–1943. Professor of Ancient Philosophy at Cambridge.

CECIL JOHN WOOD 1874–1957. Bishop of Melanesia.

ROBERT ERNEST VERNEDE 1875–1917. Poet.

CECIL CLEMENTI 1875–1947. Governor of the Straits Settlements; Master of the Mercers' Company.

EDMUND CLERIHEW BENTLEY 1875–1956. Writer; inventor of the clerihew.

ALBERT LAMBERT WARD 1875–1956. Treasurer of the Royal Household.

OLIVER CYRIL SPENCER WATSON 1876–1918. VC.

LESLIE ORME WILSON 1876–1955. Chief Whip; Governor of Bombay.

CUTHBERT BROMLEY 1878–1915. VC.

JAMES DAVID SIFTON 1878–1952. Governor of Bihar and Orissa.

PHILIP EDWARD THOMAS 1878–1971. Poet.

CECIL EDWARD CHESTERTON 1879–1918. Journalist.

JOHN DAULISH 1879–1952. Bishop of Nassau.

ERNEST HOWARD SHEPARD 1879–1976. Illustrator.

RUPERT BESWICKE HOWARTH 1880–1964. Clerk to the Privy Council.

LEONARD SIDNEY WOOLF 1880–1969. Man of letters.

JULIUS VICTOR SCHOLDERER 1880–1971. Bibliophile; bibliographer.

REGINALD CHARLES HALSE 1881–1962. Archbishop of Brisbane.

GEORGE MALCOLM YOUNG 1882–1959. Historian.

VICTOR GOLLANCZ 1883–1967. Writer and publisher.

HENRY DAVIES FOSTER MCGEAGH 1883–1962. Judge Advocate-General.

HENRY SLESSER 1883–1970. Solicitor-General; Lord Justice of Appeal.

OTTO NIEMEYER 1883–1971. Director of the Bank of England.

COMPTON MACKENZIE 1883–1972. Writer and broadcaster.

FRANK KINGDON-WARD 1885–1958. Botanist.

PHILIP THOMAS BYARD CLAYTON 1885–1972. Founder of Toc H.

JOHN EDENSOR LITTLEWOOD 1885–1977. FRS; mathematician; the last Senior Wrangler.

DUNCAN GRANT 1885–1878. Painter.

WESTON HENRY STEWART 1887–1969. Bishop of Jerusalem.

EMILE VICTOR RIEU 1887–1972. Classical scholar; translator; editor of Penguin Classics.

BERNARD LAW MONTGOMERY, 1st Viscount Montgomery of Alamein, 1887–1976. Field Marshal.

ERIC KENNINGTON 1888–1960. Artist.

ERNEST RAYMOND 1888–1974. Novelist.

PAUL NASH 1889–1946. Artist.

GEORGE DOUGLAS HOWARD COLE 1889–1959. Economist.

LEONARD HODGSON 1889–1969. Canon of Christ Church, Oxford; Regius Professor of Divinity.

HARRY LEWIS NATHAN, 1st Lord Nathan of Churt, 1889–1972. Minister of Civil Aviation.

HERBERT FELIX JOLOWICZ 1890–1954. Legal historian.

PHILIP EUEN MITCHELL 1890–1964. Governor and Commander-in-Chief, Kenya.

HUMFREY GALE 1890–1971. Lieutenant-General.

ISIDORE MONTAGUE GLUCKSTEIN 1890–1975. President, J. Lyons & Co. Ltd.

DAVID VICTOR KELLY 1891–1959. Chairman, British Council.

ROY DRUMMOND WHITEHORN 1891–1976. Moderator of the Free Church Federal Council; Principal of Westminster College, Cambridge.

BERNARD SHAW c. 1891–1984. Puisne Judge in Palestine and Cyprus.

WILLIAM LOUIS ANDERSON 1892–1972. Bishop of Salisbury.

PERCY GEORGE HERBERT FENDER 1892–1985. Cricketer.

EWART ALAN MACKINTOSH 1893–1917. Poet.

RICHARD HALLAM PECK 1893–1952. Air Marshal.

JOHN ARMSTRONG 1893–1973. Artist.

HARRY MAUDE JONAS 1893–1990. Artist.

HUGH MACILWAIN LAST 1894–1957. Principal of Brasenose College, Oxford; Camden Professor of Ancient History.

ARTHUR WERNER LEWEY 1894–1973. Chief Justice, Rhodesia and Nyasaland.

JOHN HATHORN HALL 1894–1979. Governor of Uganda.

ALBERT CHARLES CHIBNALL 1894–1988. FRS; Professor of Biochemistry.

BASIL LIDDELL HART 1895–1970. Military historian.

WILLIAM SULLIVAN 1895–1971. Ambassador to Mexico.

ERIC CHARLES MIEVILLE 1896–1971. Private Secretary to George VI when Duke of York; Assistant Private Secretary to him when King.

GILBERT JAMES PAULL 1896–1984. Judge.

HARRY YOXALL 1896–1984. Director of *Vogue*; author of *Wines of Burgundy*.

BERNARD ALEXANDER ROYLE SHORE 1896–1985. Viola player.

LIONEL DENNY 1897–1985. Lord Mayor of London.

LOUIS HALLE GLUCKSTEIN 1897–1979. Chairman, London County Council.

ANDREAS MICHALOPOULOS 1897– . Classical scholar; cabinet minister in Greece.

COLIN HARGREAVES PEARSON, Lord Pearson, 1899–1980. Lord of Appeal.

STANDISH JOHN CAGNEY 1901–1962. Rugby football player; won 13 caps playing for Ireland.

HUGH SCHONFIELD 1901–1988. Maverick biblical scholar; author of *The Passover Plot*.

ROBERT ELLIOTT URQUART 1901–1988. Major-General; commander of airborne division at Arnhem.

HENRY CECIL LEON 1902–1976. Judge and writer under the name Henry Cecil.

FRANK SOSKICE, Lord Stow Hill, 1902–1979. Solicitor-General; Lord Privy Seal.

RAYMOND RAYNES 1903–1958. Superior of the Community of The Resurrection.

CECIL GEORGE LEWIS SYERS 1903–1981. High Commissioner to Ceylon.

ALLAN BAKER 1903–1985. Chief Engineer, Ministry of Transport.

AUSTIN FARRER 1904–1968. New Testament scholar; theologian; Warden of Keble College, Oxford.

CHARLES WHEELER 1904–1975. Industrialist; president of the Old Pauline Club in 1969.

SEFTON DELMER 1904–1979. Journalist.

JOHN LYNCH NAIMASTER 1905–1980. Benefactor.

RICHARD FERDINAND KAHN, Lord, 1905–1989. Economist.

CYRIL KENNETH SANSBURY 1905– . Bishop of Singapore; General Secretary, British Council of Churches.

CHRISTOPHER BIRDWOOD ROUSSELL SARGENT 1906–1943. Bishop of Fukien.

ARTHUR DENNIS FARRELL 1906– . Solicitor-General, Malaya; Judge of the Supreme Court, Kenya.

ROBERT DONNINGTON 1907–1990. Writer on music.

ALFRED RENÉ JEAN-PAUL UBBELOHDE 1907–1988. Scientist; Professor of Thermodynamics at Imperial College, University of London.

LEONARD SCHAPIRO 1908–1983. Historian of Soviet Russia.

CECIL JOHN PATTERSON 1908– . Archbishop of West Africa.

MAGNUS PYKE 1908– . Food scientist; communicator.

ISAIAH BERLIN 1909– . OM; savant.

NORMAN WALTER GEORGE TUCKER 1910–1978. Founder of the English Opera Company; director of Sadler's Wells.

JOHN CLEMENTS 1910–1988. Actor and director.

PIERRE STEPHEN ROBERT PAYNE 1911–1983. Biographer.

KENNETH BARRINGTON 1911–1988. Chairman, Morgan Grenfell.

JENKIN ROBERT OSWALD THOMPSON 1911–1944. GC.

MAX BELOFF, Lord 1913– . Political scientist; Principal, University of Buckingham.

MARCUS JOSEPH SIEFF, Lord Sieff of Brampton 1913– . President of Marks & Spencer Plc.

JOHN BRYAN CAVANAGH 1914– . Fashion designer.

JOHN FORREST HAYWARD 1916–1983. Art historian.

ANDREW SCHONFIELD 1917–1981. Economist.

LEWIS HODGES 1918– . Air Chief Marshal.

NIGEL STOCK 1919–1986. Actor.

ERIC NEWBY 1919– . Traveller and writer.

MICHAEL ANTHONY GRACE 1920–1989. Nuclear physicist.

PETER RACINE FRICKER 1920–1990. Professor of Music, University of California; composer; wrote *Concertino for St Paul's* (1955).

KENNETH JAMES DOVER 1920– . President, Corpus Christi College, Oxford; Chancellor, University of St Andrews.

KARL JOSEPH LEYSER 1920– . Historian; Fellow of All Souls College, Oxford; Chichele Professor of Medieval History, Oxford.

DENNIS BRAIN 1921–1957. Horn player.

NINIAN STEPHEN 1923– . Governor-General of Australia.

CLEMENT FREUD 1924– . MP; writer and gourmet.

JOHN TREACHER 1924– . Admiral; Allied Commander-in-Chief for the Channel and Eastern Atlantic.

JOHN LEONARD THORN 1925– . Headmaster of Winchester.

ANTHONY JONATHAN SHAFFER 1926– . Playwright.

PETER LEVIN SCHAFFER 1926– . Playwright.

GREVILLE JANNER 1928– . MP; writer and broadcaster; President, Board of Deputies of British Jews.

ALEXIS KORNER *c.* 1929–1984. Blues musician.

BARRY SMALLMAN 1929– . High Commissioner to Jamaica.

DONALD CHRISTOPHER (CHRIS) BARBER 1930– . Jazz musician.

ANTHONY JAY 1930– . Author and television producer.

MICHAEL KAUFFMANN 1931– . Professor; Director, Courtauld Institute.

RICHARD OSWALD CHANDLER NORMAN 1932– . Chief Scientific Adviser, Ministry of Defence; Rector of Exeter College, Oxford.

KENNETH BAKER 1934– . Secretary of State for Education; Chairman of the Conservative Party.

JONATHAN MILLER 1934– . Doctor, writer, producer.

MICHAEL O'DONEL ALEXANDER 1936– . Ambassador to Vienna.

JOHN FULLER 1937– . Poet and novelist.

RICHARD FRANCIS GOMBRICH 1937– . Boden Professor of Sanskrit.

ROBIN RENWICK 1937– . Ambassador to South Africa.

ALEXANDER MICHAEL GRAHAM 1938– . Sheriff of the City of London; Master of the Mercers' Company.

PATRICK NIGEL RAJENDRAUATH ZUTSHI 1955– . Keeper of the Archives, Cambridge University.

JONATHAN SIMON SPEELMAN 1956– . Chess grand master.

JONATHAN FREDERICK WHYBROW 1960– . Man of the Year 1989 for his work on the scene of the Clapham rail disaster.

# CHRONOLOGY

| HIGH MASTERS, PUPILS | EVENTS | HIGH MASTERS, PUPILS | EVENTS |
|---|---|---|---|
| | 1467 Birth of John Colet | 1573 WILLIAM MALIM | 1573 The boys given leave to play on Thursday afternoons |
| | *c.* 1493–6 Colet in Italy | | 1573 'Shed, formerly the children's pissing place, made into a residence for the Porter' |
| | *c.* 1505 Colet made Dean of St Paul's | | |
| | 1508 First reference to building of the new School | | |
| 1509 WILLIAM LILY | 1509 Colet begins to endow the School | 1581 JOHN HARRISON | 1589 George Nichols, formerly assistant master, executed at Tyburn |
| | 1510 Colet presents Lily with the Ordinances | Lionel Cranfield *c.* 1585 | 1595 Harrison is dismissed, but defiantly remains in possession |
| | ? 1512 First boys admitted | | 1595 Mulcaster teaches Paulines in Milk Street |
| | 1519 Death of John Colet | | |
| 1522 JOHN RITWISE | 1522 St Paul's boys make a speech to the Emperor Charles V in the churchyard | 1596 RICHARD MULCASTER | 1602 Amending Ordinances made by the Court of Assistants |
| Thomas Gresham *c.* 1524–31 | | | 1603 A St Paul's boy delivers a Latin oration to James I, on his way to his coronation |
| 1532 RICHARD JONES | 1533 Anne Boleyn, on her way to her coronation, is entertained with verses outside the School | | |
| 1549 THOMAS FREEMAN | 1556–7 'The pichere of Jesus set up again' | 1608 ALEXANDER GILL senior | 1628 Alexander Gill junior arrested in the schoolhouse |
| | | John Milton *c.* 1620–4 | 1629 Campden Exhibitions founded under will of Baptist Hicks, Viscount Campden |
| 1559 JOHN COOK | 1559 Freeman examined, found wanting, and dismissed | | |
| | 1561 'Paid for taking away the picture . . . 8*d.*' | 1635 ALEXANDER GILL junior | |
| William Camden *c.* 1565 | 1564 Exhibitions founded at Oxford and Cambridge | 1640 JOHN LANGLEY | 1640–1 Gill defies the Governors |
| | | | 1641 Fall of Laud; Gill resigns |
| | | Samuel Pepys *c.* 1649–51 | 1649 Pepys, in the School playground, approves the execution of Charles I |

| HIGH MASTERS, PUPILS | EVENTS | HIGH MASTERS, PUPILS | EVENTS |
|---|---|---|---|
| 1657 SAMUEL CROMLEHOLME<br>John Churchill *c.* 1665 | 1661 The first School Feast<br>1665 No Apposition and School closed because of the plague<br>1666 School destroyed in the Great Fire<br>1670 School rebuilt<br>1671 School reopened | 1877 FREDERICK WILLIAM WALKER | 1881 Bewsher's (later Colet Court) founded<br>1882 *The Pauline* begins publication<br>1884 School moves to new buildings at West Kensington |
| 1672 THOMAS GALE<br>Edmond Halley *c.* 1673 | 1696 Perry Exhibitions founded at Trinity College, Cambridge | Gilbert Keith Chesterton 1887–92<br>Philip Edward Thomas 1894–5 | 1890 OTC founded<br>1896 Jowett Memorial Organ built<br>1900 Swimming bath opened |
| 1697 JOHN POSTLETHWAYTE | 1697 The Dersingham list made – first surviving, perhaps complete, School list<br>1697 First surviving catalogue of the School Library | Bernard Law Montgomery 1902–6<br>Paul Nash 1903, 1904–6 | 1902 Colet statue unveiled<br>1904 St Paul's Girls' School founded |
| 1713 PHILIP AYSCOUGH | | 1905 ALBERT ERNEST HILLARD | 1909 Science block opened<br>1914 Walker Library opened<br>1926 War Memorial Chapel dedicated |
| 1721 BENJAMIN MORLAND | 1724 Publication of Knight's *Life of Colet*<br>1725–49 Pauline Exhibitions cease | 1927 JOHN BELL | 1934 Biology labs built |
| 1733 TIMOTHY CRUMPE | | 1939 WALTER OAKESHOTT | 1939–45 School at Easthampstead Park, Berkshire<br>1942–4 School buildings used as General Montgomery's invasion headquarters<br>1943 Colet Court acquired as St Paul's Preparatory School<br>1944 School buildings damaged by bombing<br>1944 George VI and Churchill attend D-day briefing in School buildings<br>1945 School returns to Hammersmith |
| 1737 GEORGE CHARLES | | | |
| 1748 GEORGE THICKNESSE | 1748 Number of boys down to 35. High Master Charles dismissed<br>1748 Act of Parliament to settle Mercers' financial difficulties<br>1748 Continuous Admission Registers begin<br>1750 Regular appointment of Fourth Master begins | | |
| 1769 RICHARD ROBERTS | 1813 Book prizes first awarded | 1946 ROBERT LEOLINE JAMES | |
| 1814 JOHN SLEATH | 1814 School propped up for victory celebrations<br>1820 Sleath refuses to undergo annual re-appointment until threatened with dismissal | 1953 ANTHONY NEWCOMBE GILKES | 1957 New science block opened<br>1959 HM Queen Elizabeth II visits the School |
| Benjamin Jowett 1829–36 | 1824 School rebuilt and enlarged | 1962 THOMAS HOWARTH | 1964 New site at Barnes bought for £900,000<br>1965 Hammersmith site bought by LCC for £2,100,000<br>1968 School moves to riverside at Barnes |
| 1838 HERBERT KYNASTON | 1843 First mathematics master appointed<br>1853 Union Society founded<br>1853 First French master appointed<br>? 1858 Cricket ground acquired at the Oval<br>1859 Music Society founded<br>1861 Athletic Sports Club founded<br>1861–4 Public Schools' Commission<br>1864 Prince of Wales attends Apposition and is refused a remedy | 1973 WARWICK HELE | 1973–4 36 open awards at Oxford and Cambridge won<br>1982 St Paul's wins *Daily Mail* Bridge Cup and *The Times* Chess Tournament<br>1982 Science lecture theatre built<br>1983 CDT Department founded<br>1983 Computing Department founded |
| | *c.* 1866 Football Club founded<br>1871 St Paul's a foundation member of the Rugby Football Union<br>1872 Old Pauline Club founded<br>1876 New scheme of government for St Paul's in force | 1986 PETER PILKINGTON | 1987 George Nichols (Assistant Master 1571–81), beatified by Pope John Paul II<br>1987 Theatre rebuilt<br>1989 Work begun on extensive additions to the School buildings |

# SELECT BIBLIOGRAPHY

## HISTORIES AND RELATED WORKS

Gardiner, R. B. and Lupton, John (eds), *Res Paulinae: the Eighth Half-Century of St. Paul's School*, London, 1911.
(A collection of essays on the period 1859–1909.)

Hayward, Eric, *The Story of the Meetings 1900–1977*, 2nd edition, London, 1977.
(A history of St Paul's School Christian Union.)

McDonnell, Michael F. J., *A History of St Paul's School*, London, 1909.
(The most substantial, this covers the whole history of the School up to the time of publication.)

McDonnell, Sir Michael, KBE, *The Annals of St. Paul's School*, Cambridge, 1959.
(Adds to his *History* the fruits of fifty years' further research, but only goes up to 1748.)

Piciotto, Cyril, *St. Paul's*, London, 1939.
(An outline history; only deals briefly with events before 1884.)

Richards, A. N. G., *St. Paul's School in West Kensington 1884–1968*, London, 1968.
('A brief account of the buildings and site.')

Salter, F. R., *St. Paul's School 1909–59*, London, 1959.
(This continues where McDonnell's *History* leaves off.)

Sams, H. A., *Pauline and Old Pauline*, Cambridge, 1933.
(A personal 'contribution to the history' of the School, with material on Old Paulines in India.)

## BIOGRAPHICAL RECORDS OF OLD PAULINES AND MASTERS

Gardiner, R. B., *The Admission Registers of St. Paul's School from 1748–1876*, London, 1884.
(Also contains fasti and extensive historical material in appendices.)

Gardiner, R. B., *The Admission Registers of St. Paul's School From 1876–1905*, London, 1906.

McDonnell, Sir Michael, KBE, *The Registers of St. Paul's School 1509–1748*, London, 1977.
(No registers in fact survive for this period, but this work lists all Paulines known to the author who entered the School up to 1748, with biographical material.)

*Registers of St Paul's School 1905–1985*, 1990.

## LIVES OF COLET

Knight, Samuel, *The Life of Dr. John Colet, Dean of S. Paul's . . . and Founder of S. Paul's School: with an Appendix containing some account of the Masters and more Eminent Scholars of that Foundation*, London, 1724.
(Includes much valuable primary material.)

Lupton, J. H., *Life of John Colet*, 1909.

Marriott, Sir J. A. R., *The Life of John Colet*, London, 1933.

Mackenzie, Mary L., *Dame Christian Colet: Her Life and Family*, Cambridge, 1923.
(A life of Colet's mother.)

## OTHER BIOGRAPHIES

Bentley, E. C., *Those Days*, London, 1940.

Chesterton, G. K., *Autobiography*, Plymouth, 1936.

Clark, D. L., *John Milton and St. Paul's School*, New York, 1948.
(Very informative on St. Paul's and its curriculum in the seventeenth century.)

DeMolen, R. L., *Richard Mulcaster and Educational Reform in the Renaissance* (forthcoming)

Dudley, Ruth, *Victor Gollancz: A Biograph*, London, 1987.

Fearon, Henry, *Mark My Footsteps*, London, 1955.

Fearon, Henry, *A Lake With Many Fishes*, London, 1958.

Green, Graham (ed.), *The Old School*, London, 1934.
(Chapter on St Paul's by Arthur Calder-Marshall.)

Knox, E. A., *Reminiscences of an Octogenarian*, London, n.d. (*c*.1935).

Mackenzie, Compton, *My Life and Times Octave Two 1891–1900*, London, 1963.

Marcy, W. N., *Reminiscences of a Public Schoolboy*, London, 1932.

Shepard, E. H., *Drawn From Life*, London, 1961.

Thorn, John, *The Road to Winchester*, London, 1989.

Woolf, Leonard, *Sowing*, London, 1961.

Yoxall, H. W., *A Fashion of Life*, London, 1966.

## FICTION

Mackenzie, Compton, *Sinister Street*, vol I: *Youth's Encounter*, New York, 1913

Raymond, Ernest, *Mr. Olim*, London, 1961.

# INDEX

# Picture Acknowledgements

All the pictures in this book were taken from the School Archives, with the exception of the following:

**Reproduced by courtesy of John Allport:** facing page 33

**Reproduced by courtesy of the Trustees of the British Museum:** 10, 50 (top)

**Cassell, 1961:** 87

**Sydney Francis:** facing page 83 (bottom)

**Guildhall Library, City of London:** 16 (bottom), 17 (bottom), 21 (bottom), 24 (right), 31, 46

**Hammersmith & Fulham Archives:** facing page 65 (top)

**Dr M. K. Lawson:** 127

**The Master and Fellows, Magdalene College, Cambridge:** 24(left), 35, 38

**The Worshipful Company of Mercers, London:** facing page 16, 50 (bottom), facing page 65 (bottom)

**Methuen, 1961:** 78 (bottom), 84

**The Museum of London:** facing page 17 (bottom)

**Reproduced by courtesy of the National Maritime Museum, Greenwich:** 32

**© The Pierpont Morgan Library, New York, 1990:** facing page 17 (top)

**The Master and Fellows, Trinity College, Cambridge:** 39 (top)

**Windsor Castle, Royal Library. © 1990 Her Majesty Queen Elizabeth II:** 13 (right)